THE KINGDOM SHIFT

By Dr. Paul A. Thomas

A Breakthrough to New Horizons as you Shift your Thinking into Kingdom Truths

Copyright © 2009 by Dr. Paul A. Thomas

The Kingdom Shift
A Breakthrough to New Horizons as you Shift your
Thinking into Kingdom Truths
by Dr. Paul A. Thomas

www.victorychristianassemblychurch.org

Printed in the United States of America

ISBN 978-1-60791-859-2

All rights reserved solely by the author. The author guarantees all contents are original and do not infringe upon the legal rights of any other person or work. No part of this book may be reproduced in any form without the permission of the author. The views expressed in this book are not necessarily those of the publisher.

Unless otherwise indicated, Bible quotations are taken from The King James Version of the Bible. Copyright © 1987 by Holman Bible Publishers.

www.xulonpress.com

Table of Contents

Dedication vii

The Prologue ix

   1. The Paradigm Shift 11
   2. The Unlimited Potential 17
   3. Unlimited Prayer Power 19
   4. Unlocking Your Potential 23
   5. Doing the Works of God 29
   6. The Servants Potential 31
   7. Hindrances to Your Potential 33
   8. Knowing the Will of God 39
   9. Kingdom Warfare 43
  10. Self-Anointings 53
  11. Real Spiritual Warfare 61
  12. Discovering God's Way 63
  13. Time Management 67
  14. Now The Serpent 71
  15. The Results of Sin 75
  16. The Seed of the Woman 79
  17. Plight of Man 87
  18. Overcoming Barriers to the Kingdom 91
  19. The Biggest Barrier 99
  20. Kingdom Benefits 107

21. The Apostolic/The Kingdom of God 109
22. The Prophet in the House 119

Dedication

I dedicate this book to a man's best prayer warrior, my wife Mrs. Katie Thomas for your prayerful support and patience. I salute you. To a leader's best Executive Assistant, Mrs. Barbara Campbell, our sincere appreciation for your service and capable assistance to bring the Kingdom Shift to manifestation. To Greg Campbell, a true assistant in pursuing the Will of God. To Kimberly Norman, I appreciate you for your technical support in bringing the manuscript to order. To Nashera Maye, for your assistance and computer skills, we are grateful. To a man's dearest sister, Ms. Valora Stuwart and my daughter, Eileen Thomas, I appreciate your support and devotion to my Kingdom endeavors. And to a church that strives to move with the Kingdom, a congregation that any pastor would dream of, we appreciate your prayers and support.

To the memory of my "brother"-in-law, Pastor Wade Patrick who transitioned before the completion. You were my wind beneath my wings.

The Prologue

The Bible is inundated with the word Kingdom but just a few times in the New Testament does it mention the word church. I believe the word Kingdom is redundant for a very important reason; this is the Will of God to make the earth a part of His Domain. The prayer He taught His disciples confirms this fact in **St Luke 11:2** "Thy kingdom come" is part of His prayer. In **St Matt 6:33**, He makes an emphatic statement **"But seek ye first the kingdom of God, and his righteousness; and all these things shall be added unto you."** I believe this is pertinent for our temporal needs to be met. We are not instructed to seek first the church because we are the church. The church is people and people are temporal; if we seek first the Kingdom, the church will come. **"THE KINGDOM SHIFT"** will give the reader practical steps to understand how to prioritize seeking the Kingdom of God. It also gives insight to know how to unlock your potential. It brings to the reader a new understanding to note that the Kingdom of God extends its boundaries to marriage. It also brings a paradigm shift for 21st Century ministry. This book will cause an inferno in your thought life. I believe the Holy Spirit is leading the church to the Kingdom. Without proper comprehension of what the Holy Spirit is doing, we will frustrate Him. We can also run the risk of quenching the Spirit of the Lord. Every person regardless of their position in the church will benefit from **"THE KINGDOM SHIFT"** to broaden their knowledge of Kingdom truth. Moreover, equip them to become empowered servants of God's Domain. As we see economic downturns and crisis times, which have blanketed the world, it is the time to rise up and take the Kingdom of God to every nation, kingdom and tongue. We have been chosen by God to be spiritual marines and take back creation for the King of Glory. **"THE KINGDOM SHIFT"** will give the reader Revelation knowledge that is crucial for all who desire to shift in divine timing and precision. It is my prayer that this book will not just be another book, but a book that will transform your life and ministry. This is A MUST READ.

Chapter One

THE PARADIGM SHIFT

The awesome power of the soul will boggle the mind when we allow the Holy Spirit to renew our minds. We will experience a paradigm shift in our life if we are willing to really be transformed as a new creation in the earth. It is a tragic fact that many Christians are content to just experience what we call being saved, converted and born again. Call it what you want. If this is all Christianity can do for us, I believe we have missed what the Apostles and prophets experienced when they received the Holy Spirit. Why did Jesus constrain the disciples to tarry in Jerusalem until they were filled with the Holy Ghost? He desired to birth a new creation in the earth that would supersede His extraordinary life, particularly in the last three and a half years when He walked as God in the earth. THE MANIFESTATION OF EMMANUEL. Did Jesus walk the earth doing the supernatural, raising the dead, feeding the multitudes, exorcising demons and astounding both the religious and political leaders of His day, etc to prove the fact that He was Emmanuel: God with us? If this was the only reason He came through forty and two generations to show what God can do, it would have been a tremendous show and a blessing to those who were recipients of His miracles. BUT IT WOULD BE OF NO VALUE TO US TODAY. But everything He did was for our example. That is why He chose 12 disciples who later He would empower to become apostles capable of doing everything He did while He was on the earth. He said in **St.**

John 14:12, "Verily verily I say unto you, He that believeth on me, the works that I do shall he do also and greater works shall he do; because I go unto my Father." Doing the work of Christ as His ambassadors brings glory to God.

THE GLORY OF GOD

The glory of God is His honor. This belongs only to God. An example is if I purchased a Cadillac car. This vehicle would have originated in a General Motors manufacturing plant; it would be a GM product. Therefore, all parts and necessary adjustments have to be addressed to GM or a GM dealer. When we take God's honor, we take what belongs to God and give the honor to someone else. You cannot take a GM automobile and put a Ford warranty or a Toyota warranty on it. Each manufacturer has its own warranty. We cannot take a GM product and expect Ford or Toyota to honor that warranty. Neither can I use Ford products to fix my Cadillac. God is the creator of man, not the manufacturer. When the creation exalts themselves above the creator and fails to reverence and reference Him, we are refusing to honor Him for who He is. He is Elohim, THE MOST HIGH GOD. Lucifer committed this offence, **Isaiah 14:13, "For thou hast said in thine heart, I will ascend into heaven, I will exalt my throne above the stars of God: I will sit also upon the mount of the congregation, in the sides of the North."** What a travesty of justice Lucifer committed! He planned to dethrone God. He was God's creation created to lead in giving God honor. He was created as an Ark Angel. But the bible states iniquity was found in him. **Ezekiel 28:15** states, **"Thou was perfect in thy ways from the day that thou was created, till iniquity was found in thee"**. Iniquity is a violation of one's duty or right. It is wickedness. Iniquity begins in the thoughts. Let's examine **Isaiah 14:13, "Thou hast said in thine heart"**. This iniquity started in the heart of the mind; this is where iniquity begins its downfall. Notice Lucifer was stuck on himself, his beauty, intelligence and ability. He became obsessed with his SELF. He became an idol unto himself. Secondly, notice the five times in **Isaiah 14:13** where he said, **"I WILL"**. This is redundancy of pride. He disregarded God's ultimate Will which wisdom teaches we should always acknowledge. **"For that ye ought to say, If the Lord will, we shall live and do this or that". James 4:15.** However, we know that Lucifer could never dethrone the Creator. Giving God glory is a must because CREATION SHOULD ALWAYS REFLECT THE CREATOR. It is a law; nothing works separated from its source: the birds that soar through the air without a compass; the fish that knows its point of origin and can swim back without a navigation system. The trees that produce fruit that began with a tiny seed producing big, red beautiful apples without assistance from man is giving glory to God. The plant kingdom, the animal kingdom, the fowl kingdom and the water kingdom, they all give glory to God. The human kingdom is the only kingdom that has a problem with Giving God Glory.

GIVING GOD GLORY

Giving God glory works just like all of God's laws found in **St. Luke 6:38, "Give and it shall be given unto you, good measure, pressed down and shaken together and running over shall men give into your bosom. For with the same measure that ye mete withal (WITH EVERYTHING) it shall be measured to you again."** How often have I heard this scripture just related to money? It is a law that works with everything that we need requires a seed. You and I need God's honor to operate as God's reflection in the earth. Man has lived beneath his privilege walking in the earth. Today, as Jesus walked yesterday, that is the whole purpose of the Holy Spirit to fill us with the unlimited power of the Living God. **Col 1:27, "To whom God would make known among the Gentiles; which is Christ in you the hope of glory."** Supernatural empowerment is a direct result of God's glory. Whatever you give to God, you always receive the intangible power of the living Christ as the result of your tangible seed. To give God honor is a law unless we become deceived as Lucifer, we need God to honor us. This honor belongs to us as we reflect God in the earth. The world is on a collision course to shame and reproach because of dishonoring God. This brings swift judgment because man has a major idol that has brought about mental and spiritual impotence. THE IDOL OF SELF…SELF prevents God from receiving the glory that is due unto Him, therefore we miss what we need to harness the power and the glory of our Lord Jesus Christ. Because God said, **"Ye shall have no other gods before me". Exodus 20:3**

Shame and reproach has blanketed our world because we have forgotten God. We have become shameful, immoral, evil, and lawless, etc. We worship our technology, our advanced superior knowledge, we worship pleasure, and we worship our religious traditions. We worship the Savior but not our Lord. It is because we are crazy about a Santa Claus God but we don't want the Elohim. He threatens us because of our idolatry. We seek His hand but not His face. What you don't plant you cannot harvest. **"GIVE UNTO THE LORD, O YE MIGHTY, GIVE UNTO THE LORD GLORY AND STRENGTH" PSALM 29:1**.

Exodus 4: 1-12 is a message that we need to focus on concerning who we are, what we can do and what we have as the ambassadors of God. We are as Moses was to Israel. Moses was God's Apostle. (One that is sent by God.) Moses was concerned that the nation of Israel would not believe God sent him. **"But behold they will not believe me, nor hearken unto my voice: for they will say The Lord hath not appeared unto thee." Exodus 4:1** This sounds like many people today, we are reluctant to walk and speak for God. We fear people and their thoughts concerning us. May we never forget the Word of God! **"The fear of man bringeth a snare: but whoso putteth his trust in the Lord shall be safe." Proverbs 29:25** Fear always works just like faith but in reverse. Fear cometh by hearing the negative and believing the negative. The just shall live by their faith. The unjust shall die by their fear. Fear will always attract negative circumstances to you. God never gets glory from our fear because it becomes an idol. No matter what you fear, it will appear to enlarge itself when you concentrate on it. FEAR IS FALSE EVIDENCE APPEARING REAL. We also fear to accept the fact that we are SONS OF GOD: It has nothing to do with what is your gender, race or nationality. We are the manifested sons of God, joint heirs with Jesus Christ, The Word made Flesh in the earth. We can do even more than what Jesus our Elder brother did on the earth because He said we would and the Holy Spirit empowers us to do so. We have unlimited power because we dare to believe God's Word. We must activate the fact that we have been chosen to MANIFEST EMMANUEL in the earth. Giving God glory activates your potential.

Chapter Two

<u>THE UNLIMITED POTENTIAL</u>

Accepting Christ is to do more than help you to escape hell and go to heaven. It is to give you an unlimited potential. This will equip you to manifest Emmanuel wherever you are and no matter what circumstances you face. I believe that in this critical hour that just as Moses demonstrated God before the Pharoah of Egypt, I believe today that the kingdom of darkness will not let its captives free without a demonstration of our God. Christianity has joined the ranks of many religions that can only appeal to man's logic. We have lost the Apostolic power and authority because we want to be popular with people so we shy away from believing the supernatural. We fear demonic warfare today. If Paul the apostle challenged his generation with a demonstration of the power and the Spirit, how much more do we need a demonstration for our Christless Generation? **I Cor. 2:4, "And my speech and my preaching was not with enticing words of man's wisdom but in demonstration of the Spirit and of power". Verse 5** continues, **"That your faith should not stand in the wisdom of men, but in the power of God"**. Faith is an action word that demands a demonstration. God has always been ready to share with us the glory of His power but we have been too timid and shy to move with unlimited potential. We feel it belongs to some but not to everyone. NO NO NO, IT BELONGS TO YOU!! The potential to demonstrate God just as Daniel in the Lion's den proved he was untouchable. The king of Babylon believed after Daniel could not provide a meal for hungry lions. Nebuchadnezzar is like people today. They believe not because of preaching and teaching but because they see incredible miracles. Another demonstration where God again proved Himself is in **Isaiah 54:17, "No weapon that is formed against thee shall prosper; and every tongue *that* shall rise against thee in judgment thou shalt condemn."** Hananiah, Mishael and Azariah proved this scripture true. Fire itself cannot destroy God's sons. All through the bible, we see supernatural signs and wonders. When Jesus came as God in the flesh, He demonstrated God. He fed thousands, He healed the sick, He cast out devils, He raised the dead, He did more than that but all the books of the gospels could not contain all the mighty signs and wonders He performed. For example, Jesus told Peter that he could come to Him walking on the water. Everything Jesus did on the earth we can and should do it today. Somebody is asking, "Can we"? The answer is YES WE CAN: All things are possible. **St. Mark 9:23 "Jesus said unto him, if thou canst believe all things are possible to him that believeth."** Today is your day to believe God to work through you just as Jesus. The book of Acts is still being written today. We are writing chapter 29. I believe this is the time to recognize who we are and what we can do.

Chapter Three

UNLIMITED PRAYER POWER

Now that we have settled the fact that we are the manifestation of God in the earth, the majestic Sons of God, the manifestation of Emmanuel, how do we activate the unlimited potential that is within us? The Christ within us must be released by Unlimited Prayer Power. We must emulate just as Jesus was a man of prayer so we must pray. Prayer acknowledges God and secondly, we walk as Christ did. We can actually do the work of God in the flesh. As Jesus became the second Adam so we became as Christ did in the earth doing great exploits. As Jesus became the second Adam so we reclaim the Garden of Eden so we can become a reflection of the glory of God: actually having God's DNA. Every miracle Jesus performed was a result of prayer. Prayer honors God and we will know the Will of God through prayer. We must imitate in order to get the results of the wise. You must be willing to do what they do. You cannot change your life until you are willing to follow wisdom. Jesus was wisdom incarnate; His disciples followed him because they wanted a change, as Jesus was a man of prayer. Prayer acknowledges God and we walk as Christ did on the earth doing dynamic exploits. So, we actually can do the work of God in the flesh. Jesus became the second Adam to give us an example. Adam lost his position with God in a garden. Jesus regained it in a garden. Adam ate of the tree, Jesus died on a tree. Adam disobeyed God. Jesus obeyed God. Jesus was a reflection of the glory of God because He always honored God. Every miracle was a manifestation of the Will of God. We do not know the Will of God without prayer.

Our prayers should reflect our honor of God, our thanks to God, our dependence on God, our acknowledgement of His resources, our need for forgiveness, and our commitment to Him. Prayer should always be consistent. We should pray individually and corporately. That is why we should never stop our worship in the House of God because we can run the risk of not honoring God. Staying away from church can many times cause us to build an idol to ourselves. You cannot obey God without maintaining your fellowship with other believers. Actually, the church is to be known as the House of Prayer. Today we can find concerts, dinners, games, fashion shows but very little prayer. Prayer has been stopped in school but it has been overlooked in many churches: therefore, we have lost the glory of God. Ichabod has been written over many churches. Whenever a store goes out of business, it puts up a sign "Going out of Business" or "Selling Out". When it has sold out, the sign comes down last. The tragedy of the church is we pretend we are still in business and fool some people making them believe we are still in business. But without the glory of God, business is over for the church. God's glory is an absolute must for the House of God. It is what makes the church to be the called out ones: Kingdom builders. When God's glory is evident, there is a reflection like the brightness of a noonday sun. It reflects God so clear it's like what happened to Moses after he had been with God in the mountain. The glory of God shone so bright that he had to cover his face when he returned to the congregation of Israel. There should be a radiant reflection of God's glory after unlimited prayer. This is prevailing prayer. There is no manifestation of God until we have been with Him. The glory of God is the activation of His power. Without His presence, you forfeit His power. Prayer should not be traditional or routine. It should be with earnest expectation. Without expectation, there is no manifestation. Prayer always moves the mountain, heals the sick, delivers the bound, supplies every need, performs the miraculous in the realm of the spirit before it manifests. Your faith brings it to manifestation according to God's timing and will. God's glory revealed in us lets us wait with patience until God brings it to pass. Unlimited prayer will not limit itself to just one kind of prayer. No, it will embrace Praying in the Holy Ghost, Intercession, Supplication, etc. **Eph. 6:18**. Prayer is the activating force of the glory of God. Without prayer, we become spiritually and mentally unable to face the ever-increasing challenges of life. Jesus performed His supernatural acts of power by prayer. He prayed before He faced a situation or a challenge. How do you face challenges? In life, we face challenges or run from them. If you run, you will only have to face them again. Jesus never ran. He recognized who He was and the authority He possessed therefore He chose to face every challenge. This is why it is important to emulate Christ because the seed of Christ is within us therefore, there should never be any running even from death. Jesus did not fear anything or anybody. We must unlock our potential. You might be asking how?

Chapter Four

UNLOCKING YOUR POTENTIAL

Your potential is locked in your purpose. Your purpose is in the Will of God. God's Will cannot be altered. Your very existence is by God's determined Will. You would not exist without God's Will and purpose. God knew you before your parents ever got together; in fact, it was no accident that your mother got pregnant carrying you. It was a divine appointment with destiny for you. God chose you for a distinct purpose. He has a will for your life. Your life is not a mystery to God. It has timing, purpose and potential which was predetermined before the world began. God chose you and selected you to be a manifestation of Himself in creation. Before you accepted Him, He accepted you to fulfill His plan and purpose. Your sins, your iniquity, your disability, nothing stops God from accepting you but YOU. It is amazing how many times accidents, sickness, misfortunate experiences, attempted suicide, incurable diseases, deadly habits, you lived through them all or somehow despite the circumstances that should have killed you, God said to your soul LIVE because your purpose was greater than your problem. Your problems, sins, and failures can never be greater than His grace and mercy. Your potential is God's love radiating through you to fulfill His divine purpose. **Romans 8:35-39, "Who shall be able to separate us from the love of Christ? Shall tribulation or distress, or persecution or famine or nakedness, or peril or sword? For I am persuaded, that neither death, nor life, nor angels, nor prin-**

cipalities, nor powers, nor things present nor things to come nor height nor depth nor any other creature shall be able to separate us from the love of God which is in Christ Jesus our Lord".

You and I are chosen by God to be His Love bearers to a hateful world. Whenever we commit ourselves to be as He was in the earth and to fulfill His predetermined Will for our lives, we become vessels of potential for His glory. Your potential makes you supernatural. It equips you to do the impossible. Remember nothing is impossible with God. **St. Luke 1:37**. Abraham and Sarah is proof, Lazarus is proof, Peter can attest to that, so can Paul and Joshua is proof. In fact, when you search the scriptures you will see miracle after miracle. Now, I want you to know God would not just select a few privileged people to receive a miracle or work miracles by faith. God would play favorites if He had but you and I are no different from Abraham and Sarah. We are entitled to the same supernatural experiences by our faith and the knowledge of who we are in Christ. Potential is invested in your soul, your faith and confidence in who Christ is in you and what He can do through you is all it takes. Your determined will is to fulfill your potential. Your total surrender to His Word concerning you and your Spirit filled imagination is all it takes. One of the major hurdles we must overcome is having confidence in ourselves. We accept rejection, criticism, jealousy, and painful experiences in our past to dictate our future. We believe we are cursed by poverty, race, divorce and generational curses. If you accept any one of these spirits of impotence, they will negate your future. You cannot be cursed and blessed at the same time. A curse would make what Jesus did for you a hoax but God's Word says, **"Christ hath redeemed us from the curse of the law being made a curse for us: for it is written Cursed is everyone that hangeth on a tree. That the blessing of Abraham might come on the Gentiles through Jesus Christ: that we might receive the promise of the spirit through faith." Gal. 3:13, 14**

You are too blessed to be cursed. What Jesus did abolished the curse of sin, sickness, death and poverty. Your fear concerning these past curses is what empowers the appearance of being cursed but once you accept Jesus Christ in your heart, and renew your mind by the Word of God, and allow the Holy Ghost to fill you then you will receive empowerment to release your potential. Read **Ephesians 1:3, "Blessed be the God and Father of our Lord Jesus Christ, who hath blessed us with all spiritual blessings in heavenly places in Christ." Verse 4** says, **"According as he hath chosen us in him before the foundation of the world, that we should be holy and without blame before him in love." Verse 5** confirms the premise of our writing; **"Having predestined us unto the adoption of children by Jesus Christ to himself, according to the good pleasure of his will"** (foreordained). Jesus Christ adopted you and me unto Himself to be His ambassadors in the earth. The blood of Jesus Christ flows through us making us family. His blood separated me from my past life. As Abraham was called out of his country, his kindred and his father's house (**Genesis 12:1-2**) so have we been separated from our past life, generational curses and conditions. We also are no more citizens of the earth. As Abraham was instructed of God to follow Him to a land that He would show him which was Canaan. The place where God is leading us today is His Kingdom. The Kingdom of God represents the land flowing with milk and honey. We are no longer cursed by Adam's sin; we are blessed by the righteousness of Christ. God promised Abraham, **"And I will make of thee a great nation and I will bless thee and make thy name great and thou shall be a blessing." Genesis 12:2**

YOUR KINGDOM POTENTIAL

The Kingdom of God is a system of methods, plans and directions of the King of the Universe. In our western civilization, we do not understand a kingdom mentality. Our democratic system operates by majority rules. We elect a president but not a king. The President has limited authority but the king has unlimited authority. The Kingdom of God is a Theocracy, which means GOD RULES. God is sovereign, immutable, omnipotent, omnipresent and omniscient. No one can or ever will compare with God. No one and nothing exists without Him because He is holy, righteous and He is truth. Everything God does is always right and everything God said will always come to past. He is unlimited power and no one and nothing exist without Him. He is the infinite one because of His attributes; He is worthy of praise and worship; His glory and honor is uncontestable. God has never made a mistake in the eons of time. We honor kings, presidents and all in authority but true worship is limited to God alone. When we comprehend who God is and His greatness, we stand in awe: praise and worship should come easily. There is nobody like Him in the heavens and the earth. He is simply amazing! He is the eternal God, always present in every place at the same time. When Moses needed to know who authorized him to fulfill his task, He told Moses tell them the "I AM sent you." THE I AM means I am forever present. **Exodus 3:13, 14.** God has one desire to extend His Kingdom throughout all creation. God has seen the results of man's sinful condition and desires to transform man's sinful predicament. God promises a tremendous reward for all who seek His Kingdom. This promise is an answer to the myriads of people who are struggling with today's financial adversity and setbacks. **St. Matthew 6:33, 34** states, **"But seek first the kingdom of God and all these things (temporal needs) shall be added unto you. Take therefore no thought for tomorrow for tomorrow shall take thought for the things of itself sufficient until the day is the evil thereof."** When you put the eternal as priority, the temporal needs will follow. When God created man, he lacked nothing, he was complete, and he was God's ambassador to creation. His ability was beyond comprehension and he was the image of the creator. God could trust him to manage the affairs of the Garden of Eden. The Garden of Eden was to be the first base. God was testing Adam with the garden before He expanded His vision. Unfortunately, man could not be promoted because of disobedience; he committed high treason. He gave creation over to Satan who is God's arch enemy. Therefore, the Kingdom of God is at war with the kingdom of darkness, this is Satan's kingdom. God's Will is to overthrow Satan's kingdom and restore man back as he was in the beginning. The Kingdom of God is God's way for mankind to be redeemed.

<u>EMPOWERING YOUR POTENTIAL</u>

Sin separated man from his creator. Just as Adam forfeited his place of residence, he also forfeited his potential. After Adam fell, he became fearful. He had never known fear before. **"And he said, I heard thy voice in the garden and I was afraid because I was naked and I hid myself." Genesis 3:10** The voice of God was always welcome until the fall. Adam and Eve both ate of the forbidden fruit from the tree of knowledge; however, it was Adam that disobeyed the command because he was responsible for what God commanded. He was in charge, appointed by God to manage Eden. Adam was created in the image of God, for God's glory while Eve was created for Man's glory. Eve was made in the image of man. She was taken from man so she could be compatible to man while man would be compatible to God. When man disobeyed God, he caused a breach in divine communication, which is how Adam operated; he was God's manager. A manager is not the owner: he must always remain accountable and dependable. Integrity is what the owner looks for in a manager. What Adam did was he gave over his authority to Satan. Therefore the penalty; he lost communication with God. He forfeited his potential because he could no longer hear the Word, which is God. **"But they have not all obeyed the gospel, For Elias (Isaiah) saith, "Who hath believed our report? and to whom is the arm of the LORD revealed? Isaiah 53:1. Genesis 3:17** is the reason Adam lost his potential: he listened to the wrong voice. **"So then FAITH cometh by hearing and hearing by the word of God." Romans 10:17** In **St. John 1:1-2, "In the beginning was the word and the word was with God, and the word was God. The same was in the beginning with God."** Adam never realized his faith was lost. He lost his potential being separated from the Word, which is God. Adam accepted the seed of Satan therefore fear became his motivation. Out of fear, he realized he and his wife were naked which he realized after he ate the fruit of knowledge. He gave up the knowledge of God: the omniscient one. Satan set up Adam to believe God was a liar; therefore, his nakedness became shame before Adam and Eve were transparent. After the fall, transparency became shame. Shame causes man to run from God and cover themselves with fig leaves. Fig leaves can be education, money, prestige, anything you try to use to hide from God and prevent transparency in relationships is fig leaves. Fig leaves are superficial covering. God is the only one to cover the nakedness and shame of sin with His righteousness. Man has been trying throughout history to recover his lost potential with God. He has tried religion, philosophy, science, etc but God cannot be duplicated or eliminated. Anything we strive to replace God with becomes an idol. **'THOU SHALL HAVE NO OTHER GODS BEFORE ME." Exodus 20:3** Adam's unlimited potential was lost therefore, he became a victim of death. Death is a separation from God spiritually and possibly physically, except man receives the incorruptible seed of the Word of God, he receives death. When Adam and Eve failed, they died immediately spiritually. And physical death followed. Death visited their seed; Cain killed his brother Abel. As long as there is a Cain (spirit of self) in your house, your Abel (Ability) is threatened by death. The Cain spirit represents flesh while the Abel spirit represents the Spirit of God. Our ability to do the work of God can only be fulfilled by our oneness with God. Just as a plant needs the soil to grow, birds need the air to fly, and fish need the water to swim, man cannot separate from God and live. When God breathed into man's nostrils, he received the life of God. Just as a child that takes on the image of their parents through genes, they take on looks, physical traits and many times I have seen talents. What has happened is the child takes on the DNA of the parents. The mother and father do not have to do anything. All it takes is intercourse and birth.

Chapter Five

DOING THE WORKS OF GOD

In **St. John chapter 6:2**, we have a very interesting lesson. Multitudes followed Jesus because they saw His miracles that He did on them that were diseased. Jesus declared later on in that chapter in **verse 26,** Jesus said to the multitude that followed Him, **"You seek me not for the miracles but because you did eat of the loaves and were filled."** Miracles, signs and wonders manifest Emmanuel (GOD WITH US). Jesus would not have rebuked them if they were following Him because they were moved by His miracles. But because they were only interested in satisfying their stomach, Jesus said to them, "**Labor not for the meat which perisheth but for that meat which endureth unto everlasting life, which the Son of man shall give unto you: for him hath God the father sealed."** **Verse 27** states there is a seal for citizens of the Kingdom of God. The seal identifies us. **2 Cor. 1:21-22** states, **"Now he which established us with you in Christ and hath anointed us is God, Who has sealed us and given the earnest of the Spirit in our hearts."** The seal of God also protects the servants of God. **Rev. 7:2-3,** **"And I saw another angel ascending from the east having the seal of the living God and he cried with a loud voice to the four angels to whom it was given to hurt the earth and the sea. Saying Hurt not the earth, neither the sea, nor the trees till we have sealed the servants of our God in their foreheads."** It is a tremendous blessing to know that doing the work of God carries insurance. We need never forget **"No weapon that is formed against you shall prosper, and every tongue that shall rise against thee in judgment thou shalt condemn. "This is the heritage of the servants of the Lord; and their righteousness is of me, saith the Lord." Isaiah 54:17**. Fear and unbelief are the major hurdles that prevent us from doing the work of God. We must recognize what **2 Tim. 1:7** reads, **"For God hath not given us the spirit of fear; but of power, and love and of a sound mind."** God is not the author of fear. In the beginning, Adam feared nothing: the snakes, bears, lions, etc nothing scared Adam. Rattlesnakes couldn't bite him and poison him because the rattler was subject to him. There were no vicious animals to contend with. Adam didn't knock himself out and get stressed out. God wanted man to be a duplicate of Himself in the Garden of Eden. The greatest tragedy ever recorded in history was (when Adam fell). All creation fell with him. God had lost His manager. Satan was happy. Adam had lost his potential to give God glory and honor as he had been created to do. God created man to replace the unemployed angel, who God fired because of rebellion. Lucifer had been responsible to give God glory and honor. He was a musical instrument all by himself, what potential, but jealousy and envy caused him to rebel against God with his entire worship department. He is still trying to exalt himself higher than God. Adam became a threat to Satan. Many want to know when his name changed from Lucifer to Satan. The name Lucifer means "Son of the morning"; Satan means slanderer; Devil means author of evil-he is no longer God's son. That belongs to us. **St. John 1:12, "BUT AS MANY AS RECEIVED HIM TO THEM GAVE HE POWER TO BECOME THE SONS OF GOD EVEN TO THEM THAT BELIEVE ON HIS NAME."** We have been adopted as Sons of God. Jesus became a SON of man so I could be a Son of God. I have royal blood running through my veins and I have been given unlimited potential.

Chapter Six

THE SERVANTS POTENTIAL

As we discuss the Kingdom of God, it is vitally important to note that every citizen of the kingdom on the earth has one Purpose and position that is to serve the King eternal. Everyone in the Kingdom of God are ministers. We have felt for so long that a minister is one who preaches, or teachers, or the only ones qualified to be called minister are apostles, prophets, evangelists, pastors, and teachers. But in the Kingdom of God, every citizen is a minister regardless of who they are or educational status. Everyone is a minister to function in the Kingdom of God. We have been chosen and selected before our birth; therefore, we know we have been preordained. **Ephesians 1:5, 6 "Having predestined us unto the adoption of children by Jesus Christ to himself, according to the good pleasure of his will. To the praise of the glory of his grace, wherewith he hath made us accepted in the beloved."** Everyone's potential is never based upon his or her will. We often go to college to pursue some field of study only to find that we were presumptuous. We discover the King of Glory was unhappy with our decision. If we only had a passion to know His Will, it would save us time, money, and heartache. We do not choose our own destiny or our profession in the Kingdom of God. **"But Seek Ye First the Kingdom of God and His righteousness; and all these things shall be added unto you." Matt. 6:33** Our potential is based upon obedience to the Will of God. Ignorance to the Will of God can bring poverty and loss. **Hosea 4:6** Wisdom, knowledge, and understanding are major prerequisites to fulfilling the Will of God. True servants of the Lord always know the highest priority in the Kingdom of God is obedience to the Will of God. The bible says in **St John 8:32 "And ye shall know the truth and the truth (That you know) shall make you free".** Truth is more than information. Truth is the knowledge of the person Jesus Christ (intimacy) for without a passion to know Him we will forfeit our potential.

"Ye have not chosen me but I have chosen you and ordained you that you should go and that ye should bring forth fruit and that your fruit should remain: that whatsoever you shall ask the Father in my name He may give it you." St John 15:16 Prayer power is based upon Kingdom production. Whenever we fail to observe and do the Will of the King, we forfeit our Kingdom potential. Another very important factor is the power of the King's name. His name carries authority in the heavens and in the earth. Servants exercise Kingdom potential based upon fellowship with the King. This fellowship is called Koinonia. Koinonia is not casual fellowship; it is actually becoming one in spirit, one in purpose, and one in potential. It is covenant, just like marriage where two become one. The woman's potential is based on becoming one with the man. Both the man and the woman said I will, which made them one. The same is true with us and God. He accepted us first. Moses was reluctant to say I will because of an inferiority complex. **"Then Moses said to the LORD, "O my Lord, I am not eloquent, neither before nor since You have spoken to Your servant; but I am slow of speech and slow of tongue." EXODUS 4:10, 11 (NKJV).** Moses certainly had an inferiority complex but GOD knows us better than we know ourselves.

Chapter Seven

HINDRANCES TO YOUR POTENTIAL

MISUNDERSTANDING

Misunderstanding the Will of God and how to carry it out effectively happens frequently because of several reasons:

1. Lack of knowledge
2. Not understanding the times and seasons
3. Mentoring – because we are not acquainted with someone who operates in that office or anointing.

Elisha was empowered. His ability to walk in his prophetical calling with excellence and understanding how to fulfill his calling was because of Elijah's mentorship. Many people do not avail themselves to mentorship. It could save much time and energy. Misunderstanding the purpose of a ministry gift can cause presumption. We must also understand that although we have a mentor or a person who has a similar calling, each person is unique with God. The method God uses for some people is completely different for others. For example, all prophets hear but not all see visions. That is why we should not emulate or imitate anyone's gift. Don't discredit

God's method and plan for you. Be grateful for the call. Ask God for wisdom, who will give it to you liberally,

James 1:5 If any of you lack wisdom, let him ask of God, that giveth to all men liberally, and upbraideth not; and it shall be given him.

WEAKNESS

Weakness does not mean sinful temptations that we succumb to in which we are ashamed of and grieved over. But it is affliction for Christ sake; for His glory, it is often circumstances we have asked God to remove from us but God gets glory from what we believe is trials (tests). Many times we call it the devil when really it is God who is working out His purpose through the trial. Joseph is a prime example. **"⁴And Joseph said unto his brethren, Come near to me, I pray you. And they came near. And he said, I am Joseph your brother, whom ye sold into Egypt. ⁵Now therefore be not grieved, nor angry with yourselves, that ye sold me hither: for God did send me before you to preserve life." Genesis 45:4-5**

Weakness can be a valuable experience because through our weakness we discover His strength. Whenever we have a latent spirit of pride, God just might not answer our prayer to remove a significant problem but give us what we need: His sufficient GRACE to walk humble before the King of Glory. Paul is a prime example as seen in

2 Corinthians 12:6-10 (The Message)

⁶If I had a mind to brag a little, I could probably do it without looking ridiculous, and I'd still be speaking plain truth all the way. But I'll spare you. I don't want anyone imagining me as anything other than the fool you'd encounter if you saw me on the street or heard me talk.

⁷⁻¹⁰Because of the extravagance of those revelations, and so I wouldn't get a big head, I was given the gift of a

handicap to keep me in constant touch with my limitations. Satan's angel did his best to get me down; what he in fact did was push me to my knees. No danger then of walking around high and mighty! At first I didn't think of it as a gift, and begged God to remove it. Three times I did that, and then he told me,

My grace is enough; it's all you need.
My strength comes into its own in your weakness.
Once I heard that, I was glad to let it happen. I quit focusing on the handicap and began appreciating the gift. It was a case of Christ's strength moving in on my weakness. Now I take limitations in stride, and with good cheer, these limitations that cut me down to size—abuse, accidents, opposition, bad breaks. I just let Christ take over! And so the weaker I get, the stronger I become.

UNBELIEF

Unbelief is a slap in the face of The King of Glory. To disbelieve Him is the sin that hurts God more than any other sin: it makes of non-effect His Word. It makes God a liar. **HEBREWS 6:17, 18 "WHEREIN GOD WILLING MORE ABUNDANTLY TO SHOW UNTO THE HEIRS OF PROMISE THE IMMUTABILITY OF HIS COUNSEL, CONFIRMED IT BY AN OATH: THAT BY TWO IMMUTABLE THINGS, IN WHICH IT WAS IMPOSSIBLE FOR GOD TO LIE, WE MIGHT HAVE A STRONG CONSOLATION, WHO HAVE FLED FOR REFUGE TO LAY HOLD UPON THE HOPE SET BEFORE US."**

The sin of unbelief I believe is the daddy of sin because Salvation is only possible if we believe. Abraham's faith honored God. He did not stagger at the promise, which looked impossible; that faith gave glory to God. Believing God when it looks impossible challenges every problem you have or will ever face to watch God perform the miraculous. Never doubt that God can use you to fulfill an assignment. When He called you before birth, He knew all about your sins, failures and all your problems before you did. BELIEVE HIS

GRACE. GOD'S WORD IS ETERNAL, HIS CALL TO YOU IS NEVER BASED ON YOUR ABILITY-IT IS BASED ON YOUR AVAILABILIY. EVERYTHING WE NEED FROM GOD STARTS WITH BELIEF.

IGNORANCE

Ignorance is the opposite of knowledge. I believe it to be Satan's plan to destroy mankind. Satan's attacks can be successful because of ignorance on our part **"THE THIEF COMETH NOT BUT FOR TO STEAL, KILL, AND TO DESTROY; I AM COME THAT THEY MIGHT HAVE LIFE. AND THAT THEY MIGHT HAVE IT MORE ABUNDANTLY." ST JOHN 10: 10** The I AM IS THE NAME MOSES RECEIVED TO TELL ISRAELWHO SENT HIM. THE I AM GOD does not want His seed ignorant. The opposite of ignorance is knowledge. Satan is the foundation of ignorance; God is knowledge Himself. When we seek God for knowledge, He will provide it just as He provides wisdom. Wisdom, knowledge and understanding work together for our good. **James 1:5, 6.**

God's wisdom gives us insight to see as God sees. This is also the foundation of wealth. Wisdom and money can make a dynamic team. While Ignorance and money produce shame and poverty, real wisdom, knowledge, and understanding comes only from God. The schools that turn out graduates who never met God are ignorant. Temporal wisdom, knowledge, and understanding cannot profit you. We are seeing today our senators, congressmen and the supposed to be wise men and women who have gotten our nation in a real mess because of the spirit of ignorance. God is so powerful until Daniel knew what king Nebuchadnezzar dreamed. The knowledge of God sets you apart from humanity. Daniel knew his God. Joseph's wisdom was so superior it brought promotion to him. Without GOD, we forfeit wisdom, knowledge and understanding. As we discuss knowledge and wisdom, we must also know these are grace gifts that will enable you to walk in Revelation knowledge or wisdom. Everybody is entitled to have knowledge to fulfill God's Will. Without prayer, fasting, sacrifice and worship, there can be only superficial knowledge. Ignorance and destruction go together.

Many people desire to do the Will of God but ignorance limits their ability. Knowledge is what you know. Wisdom is the ability to apply what you know. Understanding is to understand both.

Chapter Eight

KNOWING THE WILL OF GOD

The knowledge of the King is what Satan used to deceive Eve; he said, "**GOD DOTH KNOW THAT IN THE DAY YE EAT THEREOF, THEN YOUR EYES SHALL BE OPENED, AND YE SHALL BE AS GODS, KNOWING GOOD AND EVIL.**" **GEN 3: 5** Satan planted the suggestion that God was holding back knowledge that they needed. Adam and Eve were privileged to know God in an intimate way that provided all the knowledge they needed. The knowledge of evil was not in God's plan for man because the knowledge of evil was Satan's seed.

This was Satan's desire to make mankind feel that there was something God does not want mankind to know. However when we examine **GEN 1:26-27 "And God said Let us make man in our image, after our likeness; and let them have dominion over the fish of the sea, and over the fowl of the air and over the cattle, and over all the earth, and over every creeping thing that creepeth upon the earth. So God created man in his own image, in the image of God created he him male and female created he them."** God created man to have His potential. Adam and Eve were created to be the potentates of the earth. Walking as God's ambassadors, God has never changed His mind. It is His desire to see man redeemed to his fullest potential. It is His desire that as Jesus walked the earth as the Living Word in the earth as an example; we can walk just as He did to reconcile man to God. **2 Cor. 3:2-**

3, "YOU ARE OUR EPISTLE WRITTEN IN OUR HEARTS, KNOWN AND READ OF ALL MEN." FORASMUCH AS YOU ARE MANIFESTLY DECLARED TO BE THE EPISTLE OF CHRIST MINISTERED BY US WRITTEN NOT WITH INK, BUT WITH THE SPIRIT OF THE LIVING GOD; NOT IN TABLES OF STONE BUT IN FLESHLY TABLES OF THE HEART". God desires man to know Him through us and to know His Will through us. God wants to reveal Himself to man through us. Everything must stay connected to its source or it will die; separation from God produces impotence. When man sinned in the Garden, he lost his place, his position and his purpose; that is death. Knowledge always begins with God's Will. Adam's potential could only be activated as he fulfilled God's Will for his existence. Someone once said knowledge is power and that is a fact. Your potential does not mean you will fulfill the Will of God, it means you have the knowledge but you lack the wisdom and understanding to carry out your purpose. Your will is always connected to your potential. Your will is respected by both God and Satan; this determines your destiny, your destiny is determined by your will, your will activates salvation and empowerment. No matter what God has done for you, your knowledge is void without your will. Everything God desires for you to know and do is tied to your will. God has already done everything you need to be successful in fulfilling your purpose. You are empowered to walk in the power of God. You are empowered to heal the sick, to work miracles and to cast Satan out. Your will connects you to your preordained purpose: to be the Word on your job, in your home, and wherever providence takes you. Manifest Christ. You are anointed to fulfill your purpose in the place God has called you to and the time designated by God for you. Place and Time ties you to your potential. This means God has a specific time, purpose and place for you to fulfill His Will. Moses assignment was Egypt, (PLACE)- deliver the children of Israel from bondage; (PURPOSE)- The children of Israel's faith and Pharaoh's reluctant obedience required signs and wonders; (POTENTIAL)- to comply with God's Will. The Apostle Paul stated to the church in Corinth,

1 Corinthians 2:3
And I was with you in weakness, and in fear, and in much trembling.

1 Corinthians 2:4
And my speech and my preaching *was* not with enticing words of man's wisdom, but in demonstration of the Spirit and of power

1 Corinthians 2:5
That your faith should not stand in the wisdom of men, but in the power of God.

Power is the manifestation of God. It reveals God. Signs, wonders, and miracles distinguish Christianity from Islam, Hinduism, etc. They have intelligence but the power is missing. I have personally not seen salvation in many crusades overseas until I began to allow the Holy Spirit to heal their sick, open blind eyes and unstop deaf ears. This is the very purpose of the Holy Spirit to empower every believer to walk as Christ and demonstrate Christ wherever He leads you and the time is right. Miracles, signs and wonders are never to manifest you but to reveal the might and power of the King of Glory. Many people believe Bible days are over. They believe there are no more miracles, signs and wonders. They believe Apostles and Prophets vanished off the scene, but God is still the same yesterday, today, and forever. God is the I AM ready to manifest Himself today.

Hebrews 13:8
Jesus Christ the same yesterday, and today, and forever.

God's highest desire is to see man restored to his rightful place in the earth. Satan's plan is to destroy man and prevent man from ever being restored; therefore, he would throw that back at God: **that man was God's biggest mistake**. Satan carries an intense hatred and bitterness against God ever since God fired him and ordered him forcibly removed from the Kingdom of Heaven. Satan uses man to get back at God therefore that brings pain and hurt to God. No parent desires to see their children to be deceived and rebel against them. When Satan watched the creation of man and saw the passion God had for His highest creation and the insult to Satan was Adam was hired to replace him, and he was created in the very image of God and was given an empire in which to rule and reign. How this brought fury to Satan and his fallen angels! He therefore devised a plan to retaliate against God by using man to turn on the one that loved him and made him doubt his loving creator. Satan uses one major weapon against man that has worked over and over again: DECEPTION. This weapon blinds man, enslaves man and causes man to destroy himself. It causes man to rebel against what is right, and desire what is wrong. It makes man procrastinate when it comes to time. He makes man feel he has to supply his own needs. He reverses truth and righteousness. Deception is the enemy of truth. **Rev. 20:10** Jesus said,

John 14:6
Jesus saith unto him, I am the way, the truth, and the life: no man cometh unto the Father, but by me.

Chapter Nine

KINGDOM WARFARE

We are fighting against a well-organized and specialized army of the enemy,

Ephesians 6:10-18
¹⁰Finally, my brethren, be strong in the Lord, and in the power of his might.
¹¹Put on the whole amour of God that ye may be able to stand against the wiles of the devil.
¹²For we wrestle not against flesh and blood, but against principalities, against powers, against the rulers of the darkness of this world, against spiritual wickedness in high *places*.
¹³Wherefore take unto you the whole amour of God that ye may be able to withstand in the evil day, and having done all, to stand.
¹⁴Stand therefore, having your loins girt about with truth, and having on the breastplate of righteousness;
¹⁵And your feet shod with the preparation of the gospel of peace;
¹⁶Above all, taking the shield of faith, wherewith ye shall be able to quench all the fiery darts of the wicked.
¹⁷And take the helmet of salvation, and the sword of the Spirit, which is the word of God:

[18]Praying always with all prayer and supplication in the Spirit, and watching thereunto with all perseverance and supplication for all saints.

For us to succeed in combat we need to be well informed and well established in the teaching of the Word of God. When the kingdom of darkness plans a massive assault, his first objective is to destroy all communication devices and methods. Communication is crucial for success in any military operation. Spiritual warfare is no different; communication is crucial with our commander and chief The Lord of Host. Without communication and obedience to His commands, casualties are certain. The soul is the communication headquarters for every servant of the Lord of Host. The soul is the center of the activities of the body; it is the control room of our thinking. **[21]Death and life *are* in the power of the tongue: and they that love it shall eat the fruit thereof. Prov. 18:21** We all are products of our thinking. We are predestined to arrive where our thoughts were, that is why thinking about yesterday has no significant value except you are learning from past mistakes. Yesterday's thoughts are like a person that dies, they have no value to you now, you must bury the remains and concentrate on what remains that can affect tomorrow. Bring closure to your past immediately before it destroys your tomorrow. Thoughts produce actions, actions produce habits and habits produce a lifestyle. Real faith is activated in the thought life just as fear is developed in the thought life. As you think, so you will speak, and as you speak you will receive. The bible says, **"death and life are in the power of the tongue: and they that love it shall eat the fruit thereof." Prov. 18:21** The tongue without spirit control and direction brings forth death. Man created in the image of God is a recipient of what he perceives and what he sees; the warfare of God's servants is always a faith fight. That is the only fight we have to engage in, the fight of faith to lay siege to what Adam lost in the Garden of Eden.

Every other fight was conquered by Jesus Christ. If you are still fighting sin, sickness, poverty, death and failure, you are fighting a war that has already been fought and won. Satan deceives many people to believe we must fight sin, poverty, sickness and evil spirits. Thanks be to God when Jesus Christ declared it is finished; He meant sin, sickness, poverty and death, etc was already finished by His blood. The blood of Jesus is the seal of covenant. Because of His blood, I am free from sin and the works of sin to activate and enforce the victory. All I have to do is believe and confess.

Romans 10:8
But what saith it? The word is nigh thee, *even* in thy mouth, and in thy heart: that is, the word of faith, which we preach;

Romans 10:9
That if thou shalt confess with thy mouth the Lord Jesus, and shalt believe in thine heart that God hath raised him from the dead, thou shalt be saved.

Romans 10:10
For with the heart man believeth unto righteousness; and with the mouth confession is made unto salvation.

The mouth is the believers' weapon over sin, sickness, poverty and death. Salvation is total restoration from Adam's fall. Somebody is probably wondering why am I experiencing so many problems if the battle is already won. The answer is You have to know that victory is activated by knowledge, which only comes through the Holy Spirit, and received by faith. Real faith is not only what you believe, but what you say. All faith must move beyond believing which is (mental assent) to speaking forth.

Joshua 1:8
This book of the law shall not depart out of thy mouth; but thou shalt meditate therein day and night, that thou mayest observe to do according to all that is written therein: for then thou shalt make thy way prosperous, and then thou shalt have good success.

Somebody once said what you say is what you get; that is a fact, your tongue is a magnetic force to attract what God your King wants you to have. The Holy Spirit has one purpose to empower you to become victorious and prosperous as God's ambassador in the earth. To fight the only fight that you and I must engage in is the faith fight, which the Word of God says is a good fight. Why is it a good fight? Because I know how this fight is going to end. If I knew how I was going to come out I would engage Evander Holyfield to a duel, but since I don't know how the end would be for me, I wouldn't fight him because that would be a bad fight for me. But the faith fight is a good fight.

1 Timothy 6:12-14
¹²Fight the good fight of faith, lay hold on eternal life, whereunto thou art also called, and hast professed a good profession before many witnesses.
¹³I give thee charge in the sight of God, who quickeneth all things, and *before* Christ Jesus, who before Pontius Pilate witnessed a good confession;
¹⁴That thou keep *this* commandment without spot, unrebukeable, until the appearing of our Lord Jesus Christ:

Faith is the most vital weapon that brings defeat to the enemy. It is the shield that makes the attacks of the enemy of none effect. The power of faith is confidence that someone is reliable. It takes the spotlight off self. Faith cannot be separated from God's Word because the Word is the proof of His reliability; His Word is the means of confidence. God's Word was the power behind creation.

Isaiah 55:11
So shall my word be that goeth forth out of my mouth: it shall not return unto me void, but it shall accomplish that which I please, and it shall prosper *in the thing* whereto I sent it.

Faith is always approved by God. All through the scriptures God honored people who had faith; faith has different levels: no faith, little faith, weak faith, great faith. There are no spiritual wars won without faith. Faith is the major weapon.

Ephesians 2:8
For by grace are ye saved through faith; and that not of yourselves: *it is* **the gift of God:**

Ephesians 2:9
Not of works, lest any man should boast.

Faith and obedience work together because disobedience and unbelief work together. Real faith motivates obedience to the known Will of God. The Word of God cannot ever be separated from the Will of God. The Word of God is written or revealed: Logos (written) revealed (Rhema). The revealed Word of God is often the battleground of the soul. How often have people felt they heard from God only to find out that Satan had transformed himself to an angel of light?

2 Corinthians 11:14 And no marvel; for Satan himself is transformed into an angel of light.

Satan has since won most battles against mankind by deception; he holds mankind in bondage by deception. Satan's lies have just enough truth to draw you and enough lies to damn you. Without the truth, he could not tempt you and me. The vital need to always be victorious is to know the Word of God. Knowing the Word of God takes time. We cannot know the revealed Word of God without a consistent time of study, meditation and practice of the written Word of God. If we don't practice what we know, there is no need to receive revelation knowledge. Your faith in the written Word can only be expressed by your confession and your absolute obedience to the Word of God you know.

The written Word is the foundation of the Rhema (revealed word). God will never give you a word that disagrees with the written Word of God. Spiritual battles are always won in the spirit; Satan's major objective is to separate us from the Word. Our potential is always in the Word.

> **Zechariah 4:6 Then he answered and spake unto me, saying, This *is* the word of the LORD unto Zerubbabel, saying, Not by might, nor by power, but by my spirit, saith the LORD of hosts.**

All of our victories are won by the Word and by the Spirit. Flesh is always a cesspool of doubt, fear, despair, confusion, unforgiveness, jealousy, strife, etc. When we meditate on the Word of God, we make our own way prosperous and we have good success. This is the promise God gave to Joshua after Moses death. Two commands Joshua received: the Word should always be spoken, and meditated upon day and night; this empowers your spirit man. This is actually how you walk in the spirit and develop your faith.

> **Joshua 1:5-10 ⁵There shall not any man be able to stand before thee all the days of thy life: as I was with Moses, so I will be with thee: I will not fail thee, nor forsake thee. ⁶Be strong and of a good courage: for unto this people shalt thou divide for an inheritance the land, which I sware unto their fathers to give them. ⁷Only be thou strong and very courageous, that thou mayest observe to do according to all the law, which Moses my servant commanded thee: turn not from it to the right hand or to the left, that thou mayest prosper withersoever thou goest. ⁸This book of the law shall not depart out of thy mouth; but thou shalt meditate therein day and night, that thou mayest observe to do according to all that is written therein: for then thou shalt make thy way prosperous, and then thou shalt have good success. ⁹Have not I commanded thee? Be strong and of a good courage; be not afraid, neither be thou dismayed: for the LORD thy God is with thee whithersoever thou goest. Galatians 5:16 ¹⁶*This* I say then, Walk in the Spirit, and ye shall not fulfil the lust of the flesh.**

Galatians 5:22-23 **²²But the fruit of the Spirit is love, joy, peace, longsuffering, gentleness, goodness, faith, ²³Meekness, temperance: against such there is no law.**

I separated meekness and temperance because they are crucial to walking in the Word of God. You cannot walk in the spirit without walking in the Word of God; they are one. And you will never comprehend the Word of God without meekness. This is a mandate for every minister that as we discussed previously is God's Plan. We are empowered to serve the King. Without meekness (humility) teachable Spirit, coupled with temperance (discipline) restraint, we forfeit promotion. The proud is always resisted by God but he giveth grace to the humble.

1 Peter 5:5-6 ⁵Likewise, ye younger, submit yourselves unto the elder. Yea, all *of you* be subject one to another, and be clothed with humility: for God resisteth the proud, and giveth grace to the humble. ⁶Humble yourselves therefore under the mighty hand of God, that he may exalt you in due time:

Without humility, we run the risk of self-gratification. We steal the glory and honor that is due to His name and we try to promote ourselves. Promotion only comes from the King of Glory.

Because of the deceptive work of Satan and his cunning craftiness, we need to discern his plots and plans. We must never forget that Satan's desire is to kill, steal, and destroy. **St John10:10** Satan utilizes deception to accomplish his diabolical plans. Satan uses strongholds as a major means of deception. Strongholds can be actual "demon possession," but hidden by religious activity. Satan disguises his activities he transforms himself as an angel of light. He works constantly to get our minds off Christ and put it on his work instead of His Word. He causes us to battle symptoms and ignore the real problem. As long as problems are not dealt with, they become bigger. Satan makes us fight with people and ignore his activity. We must remember our fight is not with flesh and blood.

Ephesians 6:12 For we wrestle not against flesh and blood, but against principalities, against powers, against the rulers of the darkness of this world, against spiritual wickedness in high *places.*

The strong man must be bound. The strong man is not family, our children, husbands and wives, not employers not our president or anyone else. It is Satan himself: he must be bound. Jesus always knew Satan. On one occasion when Peter was resisting Jesus' decision to go to Jerusalem, Jesus could have rebuked Peter. But instead, He dealt with the source of Peter's argument.

Matthew 16:23 But he turned, and said unto Peter, Get thee behind me, Satan: thou art an offence unto me: for thou savourest not the things that be of God, but those that be of men.

All Believers are empowered to overcome Satan. There are several keys we need to remember:

1. We need to walk and exercise our AUTHORITY
2. We need to ALWAYS PRAY. DON'T FAINT
3. We need to DISPLACE THE ENEMY. REPLACE HIM IN YOUR THOUGHTS, IDEAS AND SITUATIONS WITH THE PRESENCE OF GOD. USE THE WORD OF GOD
4. RESIST SATAN BY ALWAYS SUBMITTING YOURSELF AND YOUR PLANS TO GOD
5. DON'T GIVE SATAN NO PLACE. LET THE WORD OCCUPY YOUR LIFE
6. FORTIFY YOURSELF. CLOTHE YOURSELF WITH THE WHOLE ARMOUR OF GOD.

Ephesians 6:10-12 (The Message)

[10-12] And that about wraps it up. God is strong, and he wants you strong. So take everything the Master has set out for you, well-made weapons of the best materials. And put

them to use so you will be able to stand up to everything the Devil throws your way. This is no afternoon athletic contest that we'll walk away from and forget about in a couple of hours. This is for keeps, a life-or-death fight to the finish against the Devil and all his angels.

You were not created to LOSE; you were created to WIN!

Chapter Ten

SELF ANOINTINGS

There are many believers who strive to engage in Spiritual warfare being self-appointed; they promote themselves, because they become obsessed with themselves. They often are people who will not receive discipline and correction from pastors or other spiritual leaders. They have resisted God and welcomed Satan in ignorance. They welcome religious spirits and believe they have heard from God; all the while Satan has transformed himself as an angel of light. Therefore, the person believing they are fighting Satan all the while they have defected and do not know it. They cannot win spiritual battles because they have broken a law that Satan uses against them in ignorance.

> **"And Jesus knew their thoughts, and said unto them, Every kingdom divided against itself is brought to desolation; and every city or house divided against itself shall not stand:"**
> **St Matt 12:25**

Many people accept they have heard from God but they are harboring bitterness and unforgiveness against people. Satan who is the accuser of the brethren has made them believe a lie by the spirit of delusion. They believe they are suffering for Christ when actually they have appointed themselves to this battle. This same spirit separates those people from the truth. Because they cannot receive correction, they want sympathy and pity. Because they cannot continue in the Word of God, they therefore forfeit discipline and knowledge; they cannot fight Satan, because they are prisoners of war. How you ask? They never knew truth; therefore, they accepted bondage.

John 8:31 Then said Jesus to those Jews which believed on him, If ye continue in my word, *then* are ye my disciples indeed;

John 8:32 And ye shall know the truth, and the truth shall make you free.

God is never the author of confusion or bondage. Many people because of ignorance bring themselves into spiritual bondage because of disobedience to the known Will of God. Someone once said what you don't know cannot hurt you; this is definitely untrue. I would want to know if there was a rattlesnake under my bed, wouldn't you? God never authorizes ignorance; it is the plan of Satan to destroy man. Knowledge is power, and the truth you know makes you free. Sin is empowered by ignorance; ignorance produces fear, doubt, bitterness and spiritual impotence. Ignorance causes bigotry and hatred; it also causes a major problem that many people are victims of procrastination. This is the thief of time; it is the enemy of wisdom and understanding. Ignorance is the intruder to Spiritual maturity. Our ignorance causes us to aim at people. But I believe many people are not prepared to learn who their real enemy is and where he dwells. The real enemy that we must fight first is the enemy of self who lives within us; that's the inner me. (ENEMY) This enemy opposes the Kingdom of God because the Kingdom of God always contradicts the wisdom of man, which is satanic. This enemy resists the truth. Truth is not just information; information alone cannot produce transformation. Truth is the knowledge of the Son of God who is personified wisdom, knowledge, and understanding. This knowledge must be compared to the knowledge that a husband and wife have of one another. This is intimacy; I like to say it this way (INTOMESEE) intimacy. Wisdom begins with intimacy looking inward before looking outward. I cannot fight the enemy that I cannot see. This is the reason we need the Holy Spirit to see within us. Whenever we overlook the enemy within, we become blind to truth; therefore, we open the door to defeat and destruction. Truth must be understood as progressive. This we must always accept: God never changes, but His knowledge of truth for us to walk in is progressive revelation. It is revealed.

Revelation knowledge comes with maturity. It is like the birth of a child; it is based on time. God places man in the capsule of time. Humanity is always judged by time; maturity is based on time, seasons are based on time, everything we do in life is always based on time. Days, weeks, months and years are all based on time. Time determines age. Knowledge is governed by time. That is the reason the apostle Paul said when I was a child, I spoke like a child, I understood as a child, let us read it in **1 Corinthians 13:11**

"When I was a child, I spake as a child, I understood as a child, I thought as a child: but when I became a man, I put away childish things."

As we can see, we can have childhood understanding and we can have manhood responsibility. We must therefore discontinue childhood actions. Knowledge requires responsibility. The major factor for many losses in spiritual warfare is immaturity. Children are never trained and sent to fight in the armed forces, only in nations that do not believe in the sanctity of childhood. Children are not responsible for immature decisions. But maturity determines ability and responsibility is your response to the ability God trust you with. You are always accountable for your abilities to God because He is the giver of all our abilities. A child has abilities but has no knowledge of what to do. A child is ignorant based on immaturity. Spiritual immaturity causes ignorance to who our enemy is. It also blinds us to our abilities: it stops us from being chosen for service (ministry) to the King. Children must allow time to bring knowledge; you cannot send a child to college without elementary training. For children when they are very young, there is nobody like their mom and dad.

When they reach adolescence, they feel their parents are outdated; they rebel against authority. But when they reach adult status, they have a different mindset. Their understanding shifts, a process of time causes mind renewal. Many times our stubbornness, which is a form of idolatry, causes us to resist the process, which God has ordained for every minister. We are to understand ministry is not preaching, teaching, or pastoring as we discussed earlier. Out of ignorance, we have made sacred the position and disregarded the purpose of ministry. It is never to promote ourselves or our abilities. It is always to worship the King with service. Purpose is why God preserves us even through tests and trials. God preserved Moses in the Nile River because of purpose. He preserved Joseph in the pit, in the prison and in Potiphar's house because of his purpose. To understand purpose is to understand process. Purpose won't let you abort your assignment, but position will. Position makes you a Saul, while purpose makes you a David. Position consciousness causes blindness to purpose. When we really understand our purpose, we automatically become a worshiper. Without this knowledge, we are defectors from the Kingdom of God and we run the risk of building a kingdom in honor of the god of self. Self will always cause impotence as Samson was when he allowed his hair to be shaved. He was ignorant of his purpose and therefore despised his Nazarite covenant. When we understand our purpose, we will always walk in covenant. Spiritual warfare is never our fight "THE BATTLE IS THE LORD'S. EVERY BATTLE WE FACE IS THE LORD'S.

1 Samuel 17:47 And all this assembly shall know that the LORD saveth not with sword and spear: for the battle *is* the LORD'S, and he will give you into our hands.

Another scripture which reminds us that Jesus didn't pay a partial payment on the cross, he paid it all

Colossians 2:15 *And* having spoiled principalities and powers, he made a show of them openly, triumphing over them in it.

If every battle we face is the Lord's, why are we instructed in

Ephesians 6:10 Finally, my brethren, be strong in the Lord, and in the power of his might.

Ephesians 6:11 Put on the whole armour of God, that ye may be able to stand against the wiles of the devil.

To be strong in the Lord is the key to our answer. The fierce battle and opposition we face is the battle of the soul. The soul must take refuge in the Lord of host. The Lord is our refuge and strength, **Psalm 9:9 "The Lord also will be a refuge for the oppressed, a refuge in times of trouble." Psalm 46:1 "God is our refuge and strength, a very present help in trouble."** The Lord is our Hebron (city of refuge). In the Lord is our protection from the raging forces of the enemy. The armor we are told to put on is spiritual empowerment weapons to aggressively join forces in this offensive fight. We do not fight defensively in this war. Our armor not only protects us but also identifies us with our commander and chief. We can identify a U.S. military man or woman by their uniform. Their uniform also tells us what branch of service they are in. They are no longer civilians; they are actually the property of the United States Armed Services. They have a responsibility. They have assignments. Many times, they wear what is crucial to their assignments. As in the natural so is the spiritual. We cannot just put on what we select. We must be assigned armor by our commander based upon His assignment for us. We all our uniformed, but His assignment for us determines what He assigns us to put on to carry out our mission. If Satan's armed forces are well organized, our Commander and chief always has us well prepared and organized to be victorious. To be skillful in this war, we must maintain a state of readiness against Satan's cunning devices. Our mind is the war zone of the spirit. The mind has not experienced an instantaneous salvation. The mind must be renewed if we are going to be victorious in spiritual warfare. The mind is the generator of the thoughts. Your thoughts can be sabotaged by Satan if your mind is not consistently renewed by the Word of God. Thoughts must be stopped, examined and identified before we permit its entrance to our spirit. At every Armed Service base or camp, no one has access until their purpose and their identity, etc is thoroughly examined. If this is not done on a 24 hour, 7 day a week schedule, we can allow terrorists or anyone who does not have our nation's welfare at heart to have access. Just as this is true in the natural, so it is in the spiritual. Had Adam and Eve stopped and examined Satan's suggestion, death would not have been their destiny. Even if Adam had stopped and examined Satan's temptation in which his wife had yielded to, if Adam had thought about the consequences that would follow his disobedience, he would have said NO NO NO and the world would still be a blissful utopia. The mind operates by your will. Your will determines where your mind resides in the flesh or in the Spirit. The mind draws a mental picture; this is the power of imagination. This can be so real until it is just like it is reality. This is how pornography operates. Jesus said in

Matthew 5:27 Ye have heard that it was said by them of old time, Thou shalt not commit adultery:

Matthew 5:28 But I say unto you, That whosoever looketh on a woman to lust after her hath committed adultery with her already in his heart.

The power of imagination can be positive or negative; it can be a powerful tool in the walk of faith. Satan uses it to instill fear, low self-esteem, self-pity, anger, lust, uncleanness, etc. It is a tool the Holy Spirit can use to see visions. True faith is calling those things that are not just as though they were. You can only do this through imagination. It has been stated that what you see is what you get but I want to add to that. What you imagine is what you will attract! Have you ever heard someone say, "Use your imagination"? This is an empowerment tool that can steer you to your destiny. It is the eyes of your soul. It can enable you to hope; while hope inspires you to action; and action pushes you to your dreams. It is the power to pray effectively, which Jesus said we can do in

Matthew 7:7 Ask, and it shall be given you; seek, and ye shall find; knock, and it shall be opened unto you:

Matthew 7:8 For every one that asketh receiveth; and he that seeketh findeth; and to him that knocketh it shall be opened.

Your imagination can do wonders for your prayer life.

This powerful tool can wage war over low self-esteem, self-pity, and all those enemies of our true identity. Your imagination can help you see yourself as God sees you. This is a major victory in spiritual warfare. We now want to reveal another vital truth often overlooked in Spiritual Warfare.

Chapter Eleven

REAL SPIRITUAL WARFARE

Real spiritual warfare is never won in the flesh. How many times have I heard people express that they are continually in warfare by the enemy? I wonder what has caused this because-

Proverbs 26: 2 As the bird by wandering, as the swallow by flying, so the curse causeless shall not come.

Ignorance, deception and delusion are Satan's major weapons he uses against many believers. We discussed earlier that Israel had several cities of refuge; Mt Horeb was just one. A person who had committed a crime and they escaped to a city of refuge, they were safe from retribution. The only way the offended person could bring judgment upon the offender was to deceive them to come out of safety. The lesson we find in

2 Samuel 3:33 And the king lamented over Abner, and said, Died Abner as a fool dieth?

Abner could have lived had he stayed in Hebron but he came out to talk with Joab who slew him. How many times have we left our place of safety and security? The safest place in the whole wide world is in the WILL OF GOD. Unwillingness to obey the King or refuse to use your gift for His glory brings you out of Hebron. You will be fair game for the enemy. Another factor that causes curses is dishonoring your vows or breaking covenant. The quickest way to break curses is bless someone with forgiveness who you really feel does not deserve to be blessed. Curses can only be reversed by repentance for the sins that have sown negative seeds in your life. Reverse negative thoughts and speech. Sow what you want to harvest. Satan has made many people believe they are cursed when they are not. All they need is to meditate on the Word of God. Remember God has no cursed children.

Galatians 3:13 Christ hath redeemed us from the curse of the law, being made a curse for us for it is written, Cursed is every one that hangeth on a tree:

Legalism has been the thief that steals our blessings; it stops the believer from resting in the finished work of Christ. It binds and blinds the believer to live by the law imposed on them by deception and wrong teaching. Many times, they are taught that long fasts, long prayer times, or dress codes, etc qualify us for God's blessings. All this is a lie: to accept this teaching is a curse; no one can improve on Christ's redemption. Self-righteousness is a work of Satan that causes man to try to work out his right standing with God. It makes of none effect the grace and mercy of our Lord Jesus Christ. Legalism frustrates the plans, purposes and provision of God. It breaks our REST.

Hebrews 4:9 There remaineth therefore a rest to the people of God.

Hebrews 4:10 For he that is entered into his rest, he also hath ceased from his own works, as God did from his.

We must realize that our battles are only opportunities for God to reveal Himself just as He did for King Jehoshaphat. The battle is never ours to fight: the battle is the Lord's. God always allows circumstances to become opportunities to manifest His power and glory.

Chapter Twelve

<u>DISCOVERING GOD'S WAY</u>

Our God has a way to accomplish His purpose and plans in order for us to receive His provisions. When we seek first the Kingdom of God, we are to seek how God fulfills His Will. The way of the Lord is always found in His Word. God's way is always in the Logos, which is the general Will of God. The Rhema is the specific Will of God. The way, the Word, and the Will of God must always be in harmony. God's ways and His Will must be accompanied with His divine wisdom. For example in the Old Testament, God instructed Hosea to marry a harlot. In the New Testament, we are not to be unequally yoked together with unbelievers. Also in the Old Testament, God told Isaiah to strip off his clothes and walk barefooted and naked. **Isaiah 20:2** This would not be God's will and His way today. Therefore, we must examine every thought and if it lines up with New Testament standards, we can begin to walk in the spirit. Walking in the spirit is a progressive journey, which empowers us to obtain the same results just as Jesus did on the earth. God desires to raise up a new species of humans. We are not black or white, red or yellow. We are not male or female, Jew nor Gentile; we are spirit beings. I know some of you are saying mission impossible. But I believe the total purpose of the Holy Spirit is to recreate us into His image on the earth. **Psalms 82:6 I have said, Ye *are* gods; and all of you *are* children of the most High.**

It is very important to note how God created the heavens and the earth. The book of **Genesis** is a book that reveals God's way, His methods, and how God received results. God did not create the heavens and the earth just to reveal His power and greatness. If that were the case, He would not have created Adam in His likeness, and after His likeness, to take dominion over His creation. God could not operate in the earth as a Spirit. The earth requires a flesh suit to operate legally; this is why Jesus was birthed in a flesh suit so He could be very man when He came in the earth. He laid aside His glory and picked up humanity. He always got results in creation. There are principles that we need to study in **chapters 1 through chapter 5**. In **chapter 1**, there are some very vital principles we need to observe to practice. In **verse 1**, GOD ALWAYS COMES FIRST: BEFORE YOU BEGIN ANYTHING. Acknowledge **Proverbs 3:6**. We can see the ways of God in the earth. Jesus gave up His divinity and accepted my humanity so I can take on His divine nature. When Jesus died on the cross, He restored what Adam lost. We cannot afford to live as Adam did after the fall. We must celebrate the death, the burial, and above everything, the resurrection of Jesus the Christ. His resurrection reproduced a brand new race of people; a people who could speak to mountains and see them move; a people who could raise the dead; a people who could speak for God in the earth; a people who could cast out devils and demons; a people who could assign duties to angels in heaven; a people beyond description. Jesus was the sperm of God: we are joint heirs by the new birth. We have lived too long as sons of men, instead of sons of God. I believe we need to examine the book of Genesis to see how God AUTHORIZED PLANS AND DECISIONS.

Proverbs 3:6 In all thy ways acknowledge him, and he shall direct thy paths.

Verse 2 is another principal, THE SPIRIT OF GOD MUST MOVE UPON THE CIRCUMSTANCES THAT ARE OUT OF ORDER.

Genesis 1:2 And the earth was without form, and void; and darkness was upon the face of the deep. And the Spirit of God moved upon the face of the waters.

Zechariah 4:6 Then he answered and spake unto me, saying, This *is* the word of the LORD unto Zerubbabel, saying, Not by might, nor by power, but by my spirit, saith the LORD of hosts.

Verse number 3 God said this is the most important lesson in how God created the universe. He created everything by what He spoke. But man, He made. In **verse 26, "And God said let us make man."** There is a difference between create and make. We have creative power by what we say. We have been created in the image of God; therefore, we are speaking spirits.

Proverbs 18:21 Death and life *are* in the power of the tongue: and they that love it shall eat the fruit thereof. In Genesis 1:3 God spoke light into manifestation, this was the first thing He spoke. Light represents illumination, discernment, knowledge, and truth. Satan represents the prince of darkness. Darkness represents deception, ignorance and evil. Light should always be the number 1 priority in relationships, in business, etc. God desires to give us light

Isaiah 2:5 O house of Jacob, come ye, and let us walk in the light of the LORD.

Blindness is darkness. We walk in light and stumble in darkness. The Word of God is our source of illumination, which will guide us and direct our steps. **Psalms 119:105 states, "Thy word *is* a lamp unto my feet, and a light unto my path."** When we refer to the Word of God, we must note the Word of God is both the written and the specific. The Bible is the highest authority and has final say in all matters. It is the revelation of God in written form, as Jesus was the revelation of God in human form. Just as Jesus was the revelation of God in the flesh so we should be the revelation of God in the flesh today. Our highest desire is to be the revelation of God in every situation, and circumstance.

Chapter Thirteen

TIME MANAGEMENT

As we move further in our discourse concerning **Genesis 1:3**, we need to note God called the light day and darkness He called night. Day and night have spiritual significance, as we see in,

John 9:4 I must work the works of him that sent me, while it is day: the night cometh, when no man can work.

Day also refers to early life, youth, as opposed to night, which relates to older years. This leads us to another aspect of God: He is a God of TIME. Time is significant to humanity but not to God. He is never late or too early because He is God, HE IS ALWAYS ON TIME. God judges man by time. Time is like money; it can be wasted, preserved, lost, etc. Time is a very precious commodity. As we examine **Genesis 1**, we see how God was time conscious in creation. We can learn time management from God. He is the best instructor because He created time. Time was important to God in creation. We see God in the beginning of creation separating time. Scholars disagree as to length of the creation days. Some believe these were actual twenty-four hour days while others believe they were periods of undetermined length. Regardless of the length of these days, we can see God created the world systematically timed. The world did not just evolve on its own or by accident. God specifically set aside days and times to carry out what was necessary in the creation factor. Day by day, God did His labor, separating day from night, after He spoke light into existence, then on another day God separated land from sea. Then He created plant life before He planted animal life: notice the precision timing. No time was wasted or mismanaged. God had everything in order ready for the fish and animal life to eat from, then on day six, God made man and woman to depend on the plant kingdom and the fish, and animal kingdom for man to be sustained. After God completed His task, HE RESTED on day SEVEN. We must profit from God's pattern and do it His way; we can then have better success in life. God never got stressed out, He never had to go back over His labor because He screwed up like we do often enough. God could have done everything in one day possibly in one hour, but for you and me to see how He carried out His labor in six days and on the seventh day, He rested. God made certain that His labor was work of distinction. His labor reflected Him, and therefore He judged His labor periodically to make certain it met His standards of approval.

Genesis 1:10 And God called the dry *land* Earth; and the gathering together of the waters called he Seas: and GOD SAW THAT IT WAS GOOD.

God appraised His labor as He went along. In verse 12 we see Him again appraising His labor.

Genesis 1:12 And the earth brought forth grass, *and* herb yielding seed after his kind, and the tree yielding fruit, whose seed *was* in itself, after his kind: and GOD SAW THAT IT WAS GOOD.

Genesis 1:21 And God created great whales, and every living creature, that which, the waters brought forth abundantly, after their kind, and every winged fowl after his kind: AND GOD SAW THAT IT WAS GOOD.

If we would take interest in our labor and judge it for quality and excellence, what a difference we would have. Many times, we are more concerned with speed than quality. But because we are doing Kingdom labor we must assess our labor. Another factor is God ordained the Sabbath; the Sabbath denotes rest. Rest is spoken of in **Hebrews 4:9-10** which we discussed earlier however we need to go deeper in our study. The SABBATH came on day seven. Many people worship the day and not the purpose of the day, like the Pharisees in Jesus day; they honored the seventh day and refused to know the purpose. Everything God did He had a distinct purpose. Rest denotes the day of the Lord has come. In the scriptures particularly in the Old Testament, the seventh day, seventh week, seventh month, seventh year was a Sabbath hallowed as holy unto the Lord. I believe we are now entering THE DAY OF THE LORD. Man's labor is coming to an end. We should always reach a seventh day where we cease from our own methods, ideas and plans. TODAY IT IS TIME WE LET GO AND LET GOD. Our labor is limited because flesh always has limitations. As we acknowledge that fact, we will enter peace with God. There should always be a day that we commit unto the Lord. Saturday is day seven on the calendar week but to worship the day or worship on the day is not the purpose. The purpose is to honor The Lord of the day and to rest in His unfailing promises and love. It also refers to all labor and no rest is abuse. How often do we neglect our bodies need for rest as His temple? Labor without rest is abuse. God instituted the body; we must maintain it as God did. We must always appraise our labor. At the very end of God's labor, He judged His entire work. **"And God saw every thing that he had made, and, behold, *it was* very good. And the evening and the morning were the sixth day." Genesis 1:31**

In **chapter 2,** we find another fact that stands out about God

Genesis 2:2 And on the seventh day God ended his work which he had made; and he rested on the seventh day from all his work which he had made.

Genesis 2:3 And God blessed the seventh day, and sanctified it: because that in it he had rested from all his work which God created and made.

In Genesis 2:2, God completed His labor; He did not stop until His labor was finished and it was very good. He rested after His labor. How often do we quit our assignments before they are complete? God is a finisher. He never stated that His labor was very good until He had completely finished His task then The SABBATH. We should always recognize that we all must reach a climax to our days of labor then we must enter His rest.

Hebrews 4:9 There remaineth therefore a rest to the people of God.

Hebrews 4:10 For he that is entered into his rest, he also hath ceased from his own works, as God *did* from his.

We enter rest by absolute faith in God's eternal Word. Our labor today is to subdue the flesh and pursue that rest that God has for us. Fear, doubt and unbelief are the enemies of our rest. With today's trials, crises, economic breakdowns and catastrophic conditions, it is comforting to know we have a promised rest. Peace and rest must work together just like a hand and glove. When we enter into God's rest, we also enter His peace. The peace of God empowers Rest. Peace is absolutely knowing God will perfect every promise He has made. We do not have to worry or fret and become anxious about anything: all we need to do is Rest.

Hebrews 4:11 Let us labor therefore to enter into that rest, lest any man fall after the same example of unbelief.

Chapter Fourteen

<u>NOW THE SERPENT</u>

In **Genesis chapter 3,** we find temptation, subtlety and man's shameful fall, the curse of Satan and the promised seed. This chapter opens with Now the Serpent. This is always a problem; behind God's labor, behind every promise, there is a problem; on the other side of the mountain is a valley. The now reveals Satan is always ready to steal, kill, and destroy God's plan, purpose, and promises. The reality of the matter is Satan's anger is against God because God replaced him with mankind. Man was created to offer worship, praise and glory, which Lucifer originally offered but Satan was not created in the image of God. Satan was not given a dominion as Adam. I believe Satan watched God make Adam and breathe into him the life of God. The breath of God empowered man to be as God in the earth. This horrified Satan. I believe Satan devised a plan to reverse God's plan for man, and through subtlety take possession of the earth. He just did not know God was a step ahead of him, he was not aware of the promised seed. He never expected God to become flesh and blood. Satan knew life was in the blood. He just never thought that in the laboratory of heaven, incorruptible blood was created, specifically for the redemption of man. There was a lamb slain **(Rev 13:8)** before God ever declared, **"Let us make man in our image after our likeness"**. God's Love for man cannot be compared.

John 3:16 For God so loved the world, that he gave his only begotten Son, that whosoever believeth in him should not perish, but have everlasting life.

John 3:17 For God sent not his Son into the world to condemn the world; but that the world through him might be saved.

God preordained man to be chosen in himself, (We are offsprings of God), blessed with all spiritual blessings in heavenly places in Christ (THE ANOINTED ONE). When we accept Christ, we become joint heirs with Christ.

Ephesians 1:4 According as he hath chosen us in him before the foundation of the world, that we should be holy and without blame before him in love:

Ephesians 1:5 Having predestinated us unto the adoption of children by Jesus Christ to himself, according to the good pleasure of his will.

The Will of God is His Word. His Word must be understood as both the written (Logos) and the specific (Rhema). To know the Will of God requires knowing the voice of the Lord. Knowing the voice of the Lord is determined by maturity. Just as a child as they grow older they recognize their mother's voice. They can distinguish the mother's voice from someone else. There are so many people today that due to immaturity they cannot recognize the voice of the Lord. They determine the voice of the Lord by some prophet, or someone who they place confidence in. This is extremely dangerous to depend on someone to determine God's Will for your life. It is important to mature in Christ yourself and learn to know His voice. Rhema knowledge can bring illumination, direction, perseverance and faith. Rhema knowledge flows out of the Spirit realm, not the Soulish realm which governs our emotions, our five senses, our feelings; this is fleshly. The soul is hard to understand truth because it has operated from tradition. When we rely on tradition, we depend on head knowledge, fear, unbelief, and confusion is the end result of soulish living. The head always rejects Rhema; it also reasons away the Logos and compromises the Logos. Tradition can bind us and blind us. Many people cannot hear God's voice because they are sheep of their denomination. They resist God's voice because His voice contradicts the voice of their tradition. They tie themselves emotionally to what they believe is God. They become offended by truth because it makes their tradition of no effect. This is what happened to the Pharisees and Sadducees in Jesus' day. Maturity in the knowledge of God's voice requires discipline and separation from soulish desires and soulish people. Soulish people are more concerned with the temporal than the eternal. To know the voice of the Lord will require separation. I have found that when God speaks, it brings separation. For example, When God said **"Let there be light"**, darkness had to separate, He separated night from day, and He separated land from the sea. When God brings separation into our lives, it is always to bring about what is for our good. What is good to us is not always good for us. When separation takes place by the voice of the Lord, DON'T FIGHT IT. WHAT YOU DON'T KNOW NOW, YOU WILL UNDERSTAND IN DUE TIME. Abraham understood after he separated from Lot.

Genesis 13:14 And the LORD said unto Abram, after that Lot was separated from him, Lift up now thine eyes, and look from the place where thou art northward, and southward, and eastward, and westward:

Genesis 13:15 For all the land which thou seest, to thee will I give it, and to thy seed for ever.

God's voice will not only produce SEPARATION; it will also produce CHANGE. If there is no change after God has spoken, IT WAS NOT GOD. Change is the result of the voice of the Lord. Just like when night ends the sun shines. Change is an absolute fact when God speaks. When God says live, death has to flee. Change takes place at the voice of the Lord because His Word is creative. God's voice always MAGNIFIES HIS WORD: Nobody can speak like Him, and no one gets the job done like Him. His voice also is SENSATIONAL. It produces a reaction. You cannot stay neutral. God's voice will always cause a reaction; you will positively react with anticipation, assurance and peace. It made Peter walk on water. It made the lame man take up his bed and walk. That is sensational. God's voice brings REVELATION or CONFIRMATION. When God speaks, we receive from His marvelous attributes, His omnipotence, His omniscience, His omnipresence and His sovereignty. When God speaks, the heavens and all creation will listen. It is time to listen now and know the voice of the Lord.

John 10:27 My sheep hear my voice, and I know them, and they follow me:

The proof you heard the voice of the Lord is WHO IS LEADING YOU. If you are walking alone, you never heard His voice. We are a people who were never created to go through life without leadership. A leader is one who sees more than others see, who sees further than others see, and who sees before others do. The most important thing to a leader is who is following. You measure success in a leader by the destiny of the followers. The highest plan and purpose for the leader is to reproduce himself. Real leaders don't have to demand respect, they earn it. Leaders understand that activity is not accomplishments. Real leadership never settles for the good, their aim is excellence. They cannot rest until their good becomes better and their better produces a process of improvement. God is the greatest leader you will ever know because true leaders must be willing to sacrifice for the success of the team. That is what **St John 3:16** is all about. Leaders evaluate their followers as high priority. Leaders are very concerned about succession as their legacy.

Chapter Fifteen

THE RESULTS OF SIN

Sin always carries consequences; it never results in success. Adam never knew what death really meant. Sin always brings deafness to hearing the voice of God. Adam and Eve heard the voice of God walking in the garden. God desired fellowship and a strong relationship with mankind. Disobedience is rebellion and rejection to the leadership of God. The voice walking relates to the progressive empowerment of God's presence to man. But after the fall, the voice brought fear. Fear produces torment. Adam and Eve were tormented by the voice of the Lord. Today, people are tormented by the voice of the Lord: the voice of morality, the voice of reason and the voice of righteousness. The voice of the Lord is the voice of standard. When we run from the voice, we become aware of all of our failures, our sinfulness, and we discover the shame of our nakedness. Nakedness, before the fall, was transparency which every successful relationship must have. How sad it is to find broken homes and twisted lives because someone refused to be transparent? Transparency means naked with nothing to hide; no hidden agenda, nothing to cover up. Naked and unashamed was the way it was prior to the fall. After the fall, the task begins trying to hide from the omnipresent God. Man has been trying to hide from the presence of God for decades.

How tragic to run from Joy and Peace!

Psalms 16:11 Thou wilt show me the path of life: in thy presence *is* fullness of joy; at thy right hand *there are* pleasures for evermore.

There is no joy outside of the presence of the Lord. The presence of God should always be our desire in all that we do in life. The presence of God will intimidate us if we are immature. It makes us frightened because sin and immaturity will cause you to hide behind the superficial. Immaturity also keeps us from strong meat. Strong Meat is for those who have been weaned from the breast of the flesh.

1 Corinthians 3:1-8 ¹And I, brethren, could not speak unto you as unto spiritual, but as unto carnal, *even* as unto babes in Christ. ²I have fed you with milk, and not with meat: for hitherto ye were not able *to bear it*, neither yet now are ye able. ³For ye are yet carnal: for whereas *there is* among you envying, and strife, and divisions, are ye not carnal, and walk as men? ⁴For while one saith, I am of Paul; and another, I *am* of Apollos; are ye not carnal?
⁵Who then is Paul, and who *is* Apollos, but ministers by whom ye believed, even as the Lord gave to every man? ⁶I have planted, Apollos watered; but God gave the increase. ⁷So then neither is he that planteth any thing, neither he that watereth; but God that giveth the increase. ⁸Now he that planteth and he that watereth are one: and every man shall receive his own reward according to his own labor.

Without the presence of God, we become selfish bigots; we become impressed with our own accomplishments. Racism and strife are all the results of sin and immaturity. When the presence of the Lord is absent, God desires to raise up a people who reflect His presence. When we reflect His presence, we are able to provide mentorship. Mentorship is only for those who are on meat.

Hebrews 5:11-14 **¹¹Of whom we have many things to say and hard to be uttered, seeing ye are dull of hearing. ¹²For when for the time ye ought to be teachers, ye have need that one teach you again which *be* the first principles of the oracles of God; and are become such as have need of milk, and not of strong meat. ¹³For every one that useth milk *is* unskilful in the word of righteousness: for he is a babe. ¹⁴But strong meat belongeth to them that are of full age, *even* those who by reason of use have their senses exercised to discern both good and evil.**

Meat is the difference between human judgment and discernment. Without discernment, we will find ourselves deceived as Adam. Meat is the Rhema, which provides revelation knowledge. This knowledge will expose Satan's activity and plans which destroys his agenda. The presence of God is so valuable; it is more than silver or gold. King David knew the value of His presence when he said in

PSALM 51:11 "Cast me not away from thy presence, and take not thy holy spirit from me."

Chapter Sixteen

THE SEED OF THE WOMAN

Genesis 3:15 And I will put enmity between thee and the woman, and between thy seed and her seed; it shall bruise thy head, and thou shalt bruise his heel. This verse causes many people to misunderstand what God said because everybody knows a woman can only fertilize the seed in her womb. But God prophetically was speaking concerning Mary who would be the only women to have a seed; she received the seed of God, which was the Word of God. The Word of God defeats Satan's seed of rebellion. This verse also is a revelation of the antichrist who is the actual seed of Satan. However, the antichrist is no match for the authentic Christ,

> **Galatians 4:4-7 ⁴But when the fulness of the time was come, God sent forth his Son, made of a woman, made under the law, ⁵To redeem them that were under the law, that we might receive the adoption of sons. ⁶And because ye are sons, God hath sent forth the Spirit of his Son into your hearts, crying, Abba, Father. ⁷Wherefore thou art no more a servant, but a son; and if a son, then an heir of God through Christ.**

The woman was created to be a carrier while the man was created to be the planter. That is why a woman can hold life in her womb for nine months. She can also hold the negative circumstances that men and children many times put them through. God made the woman from Adam's rib; He did not take the woman from Adam's head, so she could rule over him, neither did he take her from Adam's feet, so he could step on her. No, the rib was at the side of Adam; they both were to become one. Eve was made unique from Adam. She was made from Adam but she was made compatible for Adam. This is crucial to note as important to a marriage the principal is found in

Genesis 2:22 And the rib, which the LORD God had taken from man, made he a woman, and brought her unto the man.

DIVINE MATRIMONY

God brought the woman to Adam but many men don't wait on God for their wives. God brought Eve to Adam; God brought her therefore she was made for him. The tragedy of many marriages is God had nothing to do with the union. God knew what Adam needed in a woman; therefore, He made Eve unique for him. Adam didn't make a selection; God established a principal that both men and woman need to follow as a standard. Let God bring your mate to you or let God lead you to your spouse. The woman was compatible for the man and vice versa. Homosexuality is the work of Satan. Homosexuality reveals Satan brought the union. Anytime God brings a union together reproduction is always possible. Reproduction is impossible in gay and lesbian relationships. Anything that God produces is always good. When God is the source of a union, it is not an abomination because it is a reflection of God. God destroyed Sodom and Gomorrah because of this sin. When God brings your spouse to you, Satan will still bring temptation. Just as temptation came to Eve, so it will come to all of us. Satan has a fury against God because God replaced him. Satan is unemployed. The next chapter shows us another principal found in **Genesis 2:24 Therefore shall a man leave his father and his mother, and shall cleave unto his wife: and they shall be one flesh.** There are two words that are very important to a marriage LEAVE and CLEAVE. The command to the man is very clear.

These particular words only relate to married men. The first word has been a significant problem for many men: to leave father and mother. We have seen for years the plight of a son who finds it difficult to untie himself from father and mother, God did not give this command to Adam because God was his Father and the earth was his mother. God set this as a standard for marriages after Adam and Eve because if you cannot leave you cannot cleave. The plight of man is always determined by what he leaves and what he cleaves to or who he cleaves to. Leaving father and mother has created problems for generations. Leaving does not just mean geographically; it also means socially, emotionally, sometimes it means intellectually: the Soul must vacate the negative domiciles of our father. We carry the DNA of our father but we must break the chains that connect us to our father's iniquity and sin. There must be separation from inherited patterns. Generational sins are real. If they are not broken, they will go from generation to generation. All through the scripture, we follow generational sins. Adam's sin ignited a murdering spirit in his son Cain; David's sin with Basheeba brought division, murder, lust and shame to his household; Lot's daughters' sin with incest started a race of people God hated and instructed Israel never to make covenant with the Moabites. We see generations repeating sins of drinking, gambling, pornography, incest, adultery, drug addiction and perversion. These are all generational sins, which must be broken and left. Men are an endangered species because of Satan's intense desire to destroy God's highest creation: the man. Satan's number one objective is to turn man's heart from His creator God therefore bringing death. Satan recognizes separation from your source of life is death. Satan enjoys generational repetition of sin and iniquity. He enjoys family disintegration because he destroys the offsprings in the process. How unfortunate, but even many Christian homes are also destroyed by Satan's attacks. Cleaving unto the wife was a command given to Adam. The question is where was Adam when the serpent Satan presented his wife with the temptation? Was Adam so busy in the Garden until he didn't have time for his spouse? Or was Adam angry with his wife? The question is did Adam sin before he ate of the fruit from the tree of knowledge by failing to cleave unto his wife. Adam was created with a will; he could have decided to cleave unto his wife. To cleave unto is stronger than cleave to. To me to cleave unto means despite differences, despite tension, and friction, the Love I have for <u>my wife is stronger than the offence</u>. I believe Adam could have been a detour to Satan had he been on the scene. Satan sought to reverse roles; he put the woman to lead the man. Satan knew this would hurt God; however, God will never allow Satan to win any victories. God said the husband would rule over the wife. Now he is not talking about ruling over her in terror and fear; it means having oversight with compassion for her welfare. To rule means to have authority with prudence. Satan today twists the sexes. Many women feel they should have equal rights today; the plan of Satan is to make God's Will for man to be of no effect. The responsibility God gave to man was to cleave to his wife. I believe the cleaving man to his wife will bring about dependence on her husband. The problem many women have is the man is too busy cleaving to himself, his toys (cars), sports, another woman, even Church. Many Christian Men fail to recognize God put man in a marriage before He put him in a church. The Church is God's bride, not ours men! But when men don't leave some things and some people, we will cause the wife to look for security from something or someone else. The women who are committed to the Word of God will desire a man that will love her, cherish her, provide for her, and place her above everything but God. The woman of the Word doesn't want to compete with her husband. Teams don't compete with themselves; only in practice but not in real games, competition is only for the opponent. When women are forced to act on their own, they almost all the time fall into Satan's plan just like Eve. When the woman is left alone it makes her vulnerable; it also makes her to try to replace the Father's role with the children which is mission impossible; she becomes broken, independent, instead of interdependent; bitter and overly sensitive. Just as Eve had to deal with the serpent alone, how many women are facing temptation today because your Adam is missing in Action! Some men are in the house, but not in the home and the women are left alone to deal with Satan's temptation. I wonder did Adam miss God, before the big fall! Where was he? When the serpent was carrying on a dialogue with his queen, didn't he recognize that his welfare was being shaken because she was being seduced? Today many women are being seduced by the serpent because something looks good. Adam could have stopped the whole fiasco and put Satan on the run. But I believe just as it was then so it is today. God is asking-

Genesis 3:9 And the LORD God called unto Adam, and said unto him, Where *art* thou?

Adam arrived late; he ate; he disobeyed God, which sent Creation in a tailspin. When the man breaks God's laws, it sends his world into chaos and confusion. The Lions turned, the bears turned, evil ruled the universe, man had created high treason, and he gave God's creation to Satan, God's archenemy. Adam never dreamed that piece of fruit would cost him everything. It was disobedience to God's will. The fruit is a type of a tithe, something you positively do not touch. God institutes some things to each family as untouchable. Satan's plan is to keep the man so busy but not effective until the wife becomes tempted by what appears harmless. Where Adam failed to communicate to his wife, Satan found Sis Eve very attractive and sociable while Adam was absent. His absence was due to faulty communication. Remember you can have your body in the house but yet not be home. Adam was there but yet absent. To bring clarity to Genesis 3, his absence was due to **faulty communication**. Adam failed to connect with Eve. The command he had received from God is written in

Genesis 2:15-17

[15]And the LORD God took the man, and put him into the garden of Eden to dress it and to keep it. 16And the LORD God commanded the man, saying, Of every tree of the garden thou mayest freely eat: [17]But of the tree of the knowledge of good and evil, thou shalt not eat of it: for in the day that thou eatest thereof thou shalt surely die.

We can see by the scriptures that Adam's problem was not physical absence; it was faulty communication. Let us look at **Genesis 3:1-6**

Genesis 3: 1-6

¹Now the serpent was more subtil than any beast of the field which the LORD God had made. And he said unto the woman, Yea, hath God said, Ye shall not eat of every tree of the garden? ²And the woman said unto the serpent, We may eat of the fruit of the trees of the garden: ³But of the fruit of the tree which is in the midst of the garden, God hath said, Ye shall not eat of it, neither shall ye touch it, lest ye die. ⁴And the serpent said unto the woman, Ye shall not surely die: ⁵For God doth know that in the day ye eat thereof, then your eyes shall be opened, and ye shall be as gods, knowing good and evil. ⁶And when the woman saw that the tree was good for food, and that it was pleasant to the eyes, and a tree to be desired to make one wise, she took of the fruit thereof, and did eat, and gave also unto her husband with her; and he did eat.

Adam never knew his absence would affect his household: his own son Cain killed his brother. Murder visited the home of the man and woman whom God created. What a tragedy! Someone wants to know how that happened, simply this! An Absent Man left his home open and his wife heard the wrong voice. God desires to reverse what Adam did, how? We must bring the Soul under authority of the Word of God. The Soul retains the knowledge of sin; however if we allow the Holy Spirit to erase our past and we totally repent, we can see restoration. If Enoch walked with God and God took him after Adam's fall, you can also walk with God. If Elijah was translated, so can you and I. God desires to repeat miracles, signs, and wonders today just as He did in the earth by men and women who dared to obey Him. This is restoration time. I believe everything we saw from Genesis to Revelation is now beginning to happen again. God desires us to manifest Himself in creation today. We must reveal

Him in power, in words, and in our entire lives. Remember we are joint heirs with God.

Galatians 4:4 But when the fulness of the time was come, God sent forth his Son, made of a woman, made under the law,

Galatians 4:5 To redeem them that were under the law, that we might receive the adoption of sons.

Galatians 4:6 And because ye are sons, God hath sent forth the Spirit of his Son into your hearts, crying, Abba, Father.

See the next chapter for more on faulty communication.

Chapter Seventeen

<u>PLIGHT OF THE MAN</u>

Some questions arise when we read **Genesis 3:1-6.**
1. Why did Adam ignore the important details of the message he was supposed to communicate?
2. Why did Adam allow Eve to communicate with the Serpent?
3. Why did he fail to be accountable for God's command?
4. How could Adam forget so quickly the consequences of his disobedience?
5. Why didn't he take responsibility for his faulty communication?

It would seem to me Adam should have been communicating with his bride seeing the marriage was recent. I believe the two of them should have been inseparable. Eve was created a beautiful woman. She was so beautiful until when Adam awoke from his God induced sleep, she had Adam's full attention. I imagine Adam really said WOWMAN!!

Could Adam's sin began before he ate of the tree of knowledge? Where was he? What took his attention from his wife? Could his plight been his flight? Satan always steps in when man is absent: emotionally, socially or physically. Myriads of families are suffering from the plight of absentee Husbands. Fathers who cannot deal with the high price of responsibility. Could Adam have had a disagreement with Eve? Possibly he was only prepared sexually but not emotionally. Was Adam ready for marriage the same way God prepared him to take dominion in the Garden of Eden? Was God's presence sufficient for man to fulfill his duties as a good husband? God knew His presence, labor and His breath was sufficient more than enough to equip Adam to be the man of God. We have to always determine that God never made a mistake then and never will. **The question still arises where was Adam while the Serpent carried on a dialogue with his wife?**

As we consider the question, "Where was Adam while the Serpent had a dialogue with his spouse", we must raise another question: Where was Eve? Was she independent? Was she submissive to Adam? Was she self-willed? All these questions must be considered to be fair. We cannot blame the man for everything. When we look at **Genesis 2:16, 17 "¹⁶And the Lord God commanded the man, saying, of every tree of the garden thou mayest freely eat: ¹⁷ But of the tree of the knowledge of good and evil, thou shalt not eat of it: for in the day that thou eatest, thereof thou shalt surely die."** This was a direct command from God to Adam. Eve could have decided on her own to converse with the Serpent. The independent spirit has been a major factor in marital dysfunction. The present world system has authorized THE FEMINIST MOVE: which has become another kingdom competing against the Kingdom of God. This movement forms an alliance with the lesbian movement. This movement rebels against God. **"For rebellion is as the sin of witchcraft and stubbornness is as iniquity and idolatry. Because thou has rejected the word of the Lord, he hath also rejected thee from being king." I Sam. 15:23** How many homes have been destroyed by witchcraft because the wife chooses not to subject herself to her own husband? They will subject themselves to their employer because of mammon. Many women feel my husband is too slow for me so I have to move on. God has never intended the woman to take on a masculine spirit: a spirit that rejects authority. Regardless of the husband's slowness, weakness and sinfulness, the wife should always honor her husband by grace. Grace always abounds over sin. **Romans 5:20 "Moreover the law entered, that the offence might abound. But where sin abounded, grace did much more abound."** Many times women place more attention on the adorning of the exterior while the interior is of priority. Subjection is the key to releasing God or releasing self. Meekness and a quiet spirit actually beautify the woman. **I Peter 3:1-5 Verse 6** is also very important to building a strong marriage. This verse states the responsibility of the man is to dwell with them according to knowledge. Ignorance has brought conflict, confusion and separation. This is Man's responsibility which He must do-DWELL WITH THE SPOUSE ACCORDING TO KNOWLEDGE. Note knowledge is the foundation of unity and honor in the Kingdom.

Chapter Eighteen

OVERCOMING BARRIERS TO THE KINGDOM

Jesus said, "The Kingdom of God is within you!" Another scripture says, "The Kingdom of God is at hand! The Kingdom of God is near". The Kingdom of God is the message of the gospel. We preach the gospel of salvation while Jesus preached the message of the Kingdom. Jesus did not say seek first salvation; he placed the Kingdom as priority one. John the Baptist preached the Kingdom is at hand just prior to the coming of Jesus. When Jesus arrived on the scene, He taught Kingdom parables and Kingdom theology. Jesus was a live demonstration of the Kingdom of God. He practiced the principals of the Kingdom, He lived out the instructions of the Kingdom; His attitudes and purposes were all Kingdom based. In Jesus' prayer in

> **Luke 11:2 And he said unto them, When ye pray, say, Our Father which art in heaven, Hallowed be thy name. Thy kingdom come. Thy will be done, as in heaven, so in earth.**

Jesus' passion for the Kingdom was manifested in His prayer. Why has the Kingdom been misunderstood? Why has the church put more emphasis on the trivial, rather than the eternal? Religion has been a major barrier to the Kingdom of God. The Kingdom is kept locked away for the future, when the Kingdom of God is necessary for the present. Mankind has built personal kingdoms: political, scientific, educational, philosophical, entertainment and sports. All of these are necessary for a civilization. However, religious teaching has never seen these important entities to be a part of the Kingdom of God. Wrong teaching has only seen the Kingdom of God escaping the earth and moving to heaven. We fail to comprehend the Kingdom of God as a priority message for politicians; it has a relevant message for educators; God wants to be King of the earth not king of the spiritual arenas of the world. Satan has deceptively planted thorns in our teaching. There are many politicians who believe the church and politics should be separated; this is another barrier to set up a separate kingdom for the politicians who seek to make of no effect the principals of the Kingdom of God. Secular humanism is striving to promote this message, which accepts anti-Christian philosophies, which separates God from His creation. This ungodly teaching accepts homosexuality, abortion, etc and it teaches the big bang theory as a fact. This teaching is damnable and contrary to the Kingdom of God. This teaching brings judgment to our Nation. I believe the economic crisis we are presently seeing is part of that judgment. The New Orleans catastrophe was a judgment. I believe event after event is happening to warn us that the The King is coming. Jesus was a herald of the Kingdom of God.

Matthew 24:4-14 (The Message)
4-8 Jesus said, "Watch out for doomsday deceivers. Many leaders are going to show up with forged identities, claiming, 'I am Christ, the Messiah.' They will deceive a lot of people. When reports come in of wars and rumored wars, keep your head and don't panic. This is routine history; this is no sign of the end. Nation will fight nation and ruler fight ruler, over and over. Famines and earthquakes will occur in various places. This is nothing compared to what is coming.

⁹⁻¹⁰"They are going to throw you to the wolves and kill you, everyone hating you because you carry my name. And then, going from bad to worse, it will be dog-eat-dog, everyone at each other's throat, everyone hating each other.

¹¹⁻¹²"In the confusion, lying preachers will come forward and deceive a lot of people. For many others, the overwhelming spread of evil will do them in—nothing left of their love but a mound of ashes.

¹³⁻¹⁴"Staying with it—that's what God requires. Stay with it to the end. You won't be sorry, and you'll be saved. All during this time, the good news—the Message of the kingdom—will be preached all over the world, a witness staked out in every country. And then the end will come.

This should be our message today as we have been chosen as ambassadors of the Kingdom today. This message is never accepted with joy. The wise men when they told Herod about the birth of the King of the Jews, he sought to kill them. The wise men were warned by God to return home another way because of Herod's rage and insane jealousy. People today might not be as evil and unjust as King Herod but they still seek to silence the voice of the Kingdom of God. They assassinate characters of the servants of God. They disrespect God's Servants and hurl insults at them. I believe this is mild mistreatment comparing and preparing us for what's coming. Persecution is a prophetical warning; I believe the Kingdom of God is the message that the Holy Spirit is empowering today. I believe that the arms of Moses were lifted up by Aaron and Hur for Israel's victory. I believe the Holy Spirit is holding the arms of Kingdom of God leaders today so we then can see a corporate move of God. The Kingdom of God is at hand; there has never been a time when it was not at hand. The message referring to the Kingdom being at hand is referring to the fact The Kingdom of God is touchable: it is within your grasp.

The Kingdom Shift

Matthew 4:17 From that time Jesus began to preach, and to say, Repent: for the kingdom of heaven is at hand.

John the Baptist pointed prophetically to the Kingdom; Jesus came to demonstrate the Kingdom. The Apostles pointed historically back to the fulfillment of the coming Kingdom of God. The Holy Spirit exalts the present establishment of the Kingdom of God. For years, I thought I was just supposed to preach Jesus until The Holy Spirit revealed to me that Jesus himself preached the Kingdom of God. I want to show another time in scripture when Jesus spoke about being close to the Kingdom of God. Read

Mark 12:28-34 [28]And one of the scribes came, and having heard them reasoning together, and perceiving that he had answered them well, asked him, Which is the first commandment of all? [29]And Jesus answered him, The first of all the commandments *is*, Hear, O Israel; The Lord our God is one Lord: [30]And thou shalt love the Lord thy God with all thy heart, and with all thy soul, and with all thy mind, and with all thy strength: this *is* the first commandment. [31]And the second *is* like, *namely* this, Thou shalt love thy neighbour as thyself. There is none other commandment greater than these. [32]And the scribe said unto him, Well, Master, thou hast said the truth: for there is one God; and there is none other but he: [33]And to love him with all the heart, and with all the understanding, and with all the soul, and with all the strength, and to love *his* neighbour as himself, is more than all whole burnt offerings and sacrifices. [34]And when Jesus saw that he answered discreetly, he said unto him, Thou art not far from the kingdom of God. And no man after that durst ask him *any question*.

Jesus said the first commandment is "to love God" and the second commandment is "to love your neighbor as yourself." The scribe was standing at the entrance of the Kingdom because he had made it a practice to obey these commands. However standing at the entrance is not going in; there are many people who would go in but they have a major problem with the law of obedience. Read

> **Matthew 23:1-13** **¹Then spake Jesus to the multitude, and to his disciples, ²Saying, The scribes and the Pharisees sit in Moses' seat: ³All therefore whatsoever they bid you observe, *that* observe and do; but do not ye after their works: for they say, and do not. ⁴For they bind heavy burdens and grievous to be borne, and lay *them* on men's shoulders; but they *themselves* will not move them with one of their fingers. ⁵But all their works they do for to be seen of men: they make broad their phylacteries, and enlarge the borders of their garments, ⁶And love the uppermost rooms at feasts, and the chief seats in the synagogues, ⁷And greetings in the markets, and to be called of men, Rabbi, Rabbi. ⁸But be not ye called Rabbi: for one is your Master, *even* Christ; and all ye are brethren. ⁹And call no *man* your father upon the earth: for one is your Father, which is in heaven. ¹⁰Neither be ye called maters: for one is your Master, *even* Christ. ¹¹But he that is greatest among you shall be your servant. ¹²And whosoever shall exalt himself shall be abased; and he that shall humble himself shall be exalted.**
> **¹³But woe unto you, scribes and Pharisees, hypocrites! for ye shut up the kingdom of heaven against men: for ye neither go in *yourselves*, neither suffer ye them that are entering to go in.**

Jesus had numerous confrontations with the scribes and the Pharisees. Today we still have scribes and Pharisees, they sit in the seat of Moses, and they still have difficulty in accepting Kingdom truth over institutionalized religion. The message of the Kingdom is life changing; it can change the world system. The Scribes and Pharisees majored in works but their works were done for the praise of men. They exalted themselves and all their accomplishments. They despised the prophets who spoke contrary to their practices. Today the Kingdom of God is barricaded by institutionalized religion; they pride themselves in their own labor. The Kingdom has not come because of organized religion that makes of no effect the truth. Many people stop pursuing the Kingdom of God because they are too busy building their own. They cannot accept truth because their tradition is more appealing to their flesh. Institutionalized religion can bury itself in inundated labor. Church work can keep you busy but being busy does not mean productivity. If the King has not authorized your labor, it is futile. The scribes and Pharisees did not accept Jesus as God in the Flesh because His flesh caused them to doubt. They were familiar with His flesh, but not who He was in the flesh. Today we still have problems accepting people because their treasure is in earthen vessels (clay pots). Jesus couldn't do any mighty miracles among His own people because His flesh was too familiar to them.

Another barrier to the Kingdom is dullness of hearing. When Jesus was baptized by John the Baptist, The Holy Spirit descended upon Him and said what is an all-important factor in Kingdom Revelation "HEAR YE HIM." Today the Holy Spirit is still repeating that same commandment to this generation. Another barrier is lack of unity in the body

Psalms 133:1-3 ¹Behold, how good and how pleasant *it is* **for brethren to dwell together in unity!**
² *It is* **like the precious ointment upon the head, that ran down upon the beard,** *even* **Aaron's beard: that went down to the skirts of his garments;**
³ As the dew of Hermon, *and as the dew* **that descended upon the mountains of Zion: for there the LORD commanded the blessing,** *even* **life for evermore.**

Jesus prayed for unity in

John 17:20 Neither pray I for these alone, but for them also which shall believe on me through their word;

John 17:21 That they all may be one; as thou, Father, *art* in me, and I in thee, that they also may be one in us: that the world may believe that thou hast sent me.

The lack of unity prevents Kingdom manifestation; this was a hindrance in Jesus' day. And today, it still presents a barrier. Jesus had to confront His disciples because of no unity. In Paul's day, he confronted the church at Corinth because of no unity.

1 Corinthians 1:10 Now I beseech you, brethren, by the name of our Lord Jesus Christ, that ye all speak the same thing, and *that* there be no divisions among you; but *that* ye be perfectly joined together in the same mind and in the same judgment.

Another barrier that must be moved is religious tradition. The Scribes and the Pharisees could not accept Jesus because His earthly lineage. There is no racial divide in the Kingdom of God. There is no superior race. No race is inferior to another race. We must get rid of our prejudices: spiritual and natural. We cannot see the Kingdom in a prejudiced church. Another barrier is denominational barriers. This is also spiritual prejudice that must be confronted. God has no label on His church; denominations have done more to separate a people who God has chosen but because they are not of our group or our conference, we cannot accept them. The Kingdom of God is not Pentecostal, Baptist, Methodist, Episcopal, Lutheran or Roman Catholic, etc. The Kingdom of God must be demonstrated where no barriers are. Even Apostolic Churches have their prejudices. We have exalted titles, which hinders the Kingdom because pride raises its ugly head.

Another barrier is carnality, which we discussed earlier as immaturity,

1 Corinthians 3:1-4 ¹And I, brethren, could not speak unto you as unto spiritual, but as unto carnal, *even* as unto babes in Christ. ²I have fed you with milk, and not with meat: for hitherto ye were not able *to bear it*, neither

yet now are ye able. ³For ye are yet carnal: for whereas *there is* among you envying, and strife, and divisions, are ye not carnal, and walk as men? ⁴For while one saith, I am of Paul; and another, I *am* of Apollos; are ye not carnal?

Chapter Nineteen

THE BIGGEST BARRIER

I believe the biggest barrier is a rapture mentality. This mentality only prepares us to fly away some glad morning. This mentality separates the church's purpose; it puts only leaving on our minds. Seeking first the Kingdom of God does not mean seeking for heaven. Heaven should not be sought for; it is not the empowerment of God's purpose for Mankind. The Kingdom of God is within us: not heaven. Heaven is not within reach. You have to die to touch heaven but you have to live to touch the Kingdom of God. God desires His reign in heaven to extend into the earth. Heaven has never experienced poverty, chaos and confusion. Earth has had her share of hell on earth. God wants His system to take the earth over. God desired the Nation of Israel to bring forth the Kingdom of God but Israel never accepted this Man who fed them, healed their sick, and raised their dead as He did Lazarus. They reject that Jesus Christ was and is their Messiah. Their rejection opened the door for the church to restore the Kingdom of God to planet earth as it was before the fall of man. But the church as a whole has relinquished her passionate pursuit for the Kingdom of God. We have become earthly, fleshly, and spiritually bankrupt. God is at present calling a people out of the institutionalized church into an Apostolic mindset and mentality.

St. John 1:11-12 ‍‍‍‍‍‍‍‍‍‍‍‍‍‍‍‍[11]He came unto his own, and his own received him not. [12]But as many as received him, to them

gave he power to become the sons of God, even to them that believe on his name:

Eph. 2:19-22 **¹⁹Now therefore ye are no more strangers and foreigners, but fellowcitizens with the saints, and of the household of God;**
²⁰And are built upon the foundation of the apostles and prophets, Jesus Christ himself being the chief corner stone;
²¹In whom all the building fitly framed together groweth unto an holy temple in the Lord:
²²In whom ye also are builded together for an habitation of God through the Spirit.

An Apostolic Ministry is to bring honor and glory to its head: Jesus Christ. However, the Apostolic church exists to fulfill two purposes. **Evangelism**, for too long, the institutionalized church has only seen Evangelism as bringing souls to Christ. This is not however the mandate of the Kingdom of God. We must bring souls into the Kingdom of God; therefore, they will be brought to Christ in the process. God has a program for the world. It is not just to see Men and Women born again spiritually but bankrupt socially, politically and emotionally. We are prepared for heaven and totally unprepared to bring the Kingdom of God into the earth. We are prepared to escape but not to live abundantly in the earth. The second purpose beside Evangelism is to "**teach all nations, baptizing them in the name of the Father, and of the Son, and of the Holy Ghost**," We have only seen this scripture fulfilled in water. There are many people who have experienced water baptism but not experienced the total emergence into the Kingdom of God: baptism into Kingdom laws and principals regarding Kingdom of God allegiance and baptized into Christ becoming one with God. A head without a body is a corpse. The union of Christ and His Church is being officiated by the Holy Spirit. This union is more than a one-day ceremony, as we look for in a wedding ceremony; this union is a process. I believe we have wedding ceremonies but little time spent in preparation for becoming one. We invest in the wedding ceremony but no investment for the marriage. The more time is invested in becoming one, the more quality is put into the relationship. This union is being orchestrated by the Holy Spirit and the major responsibility is preparing the Body for this glorious celebration. Just as God brought Eve to Adam so, the Holy Spirit will bring the church to Christ for consummation. Baptism is an outward expression of this union. The Father, Son, and Holy Spirit are titles but One Lord. He is the bridegroom. The Kingdom of God is the reigning Authority and power of God. The Kingdom of Heaven is where God dwells. God has a determined will to take back creation and restore it as He planned it in the beginning.

> **Psalms 47:1-9** [1] **O clap your hands, all ye people; shout unto God with the voice of triumph.**
> [2] **For the LORD most high** *is* **terrible;** *he is* **a great King over all the earth.**
> [3] **He shall subdue the people under us, and the nations under our feet.**
> [4] **He shall choose our inheritance for us, the excellency of Jacob whom he loved.**
> *Selah*
> [5] **God is gone up with a shout, the LORD with the sound of a trumpet.**
> [6] **Sing praises to God, sing praises: sing praises unto our King, sing praises.**
> [7] **For God** *is* **the King of all the earth: sing ye praises with understanding.**
> [8] **God reigneth over the heathen: God sitteth upon the throne of his holiness.**
> [9] **The princes of the people are gathered together,** *even* **the people of the God of Abraham:**
> **for the shields of the earth** *belong* **unto God: he is greatly exalted.**

God created the earth for man. And after the judgment of sin and Satan, He will create new heavens and a new earth. **Isaiah 65:17**

Rev. 21:1-8 ¹And I saw a new heaven and a new earth: for the first heaven and the first earth were passed away; and there was no more sea.
²And I John saw the holy city, new Jerusalem, coming down from God out of heaven, prepared as a bride adorned for her husband.
³And I heard a great voice out of heaven saying, Behold, the tabernacle of God is with men, and he will dwell with them, and they shall be his people, and God himself shall be with them, and be their God.
⁴And God shall wipe away all tears from their eyes; and there shall be no more death, neither sorrow, nor crying, neither shall there be any more pain: for the former things are passed away.
⁵And he that sat upon the throne said, Behold, I make all things new. And he said unto me, Write: for these words are true and faithful.
⁶And he said unto me, It is done. I am Alpha and Omega, the beginning and the end. I will give unto him that is athirst of the fountain of the water of life freely.
⁷He that overcometh shall inherit all things; and I will be his God, and he shall be my son.
⁸But the fearful, and unbelieving, and the abominable, and murderers, and whoremongers, and sorcerers, and idolaters, and all liars, shall have their part in the lake which burneth with fire and brimstone: which is the second death.

Psalms 25:12-13 ¹²What man *is* he that feareth the LORD? him shall he teach in the way *that* he shall choose.
¹³ His soul shall dwell at ease; and his seed shall inherit the earth.

Many people feel that with so many nations having nuclear weapons and weapons of mass destruction that one day man is going to end the world by destroying the earth. But the bible does not teach that,

Psalms 104:35 Let the sinners be consumed out of the earth, and let the wicked be no more. Bless thou the LORD, O my soul. Praise ye the LORD

Ecclesiastes 1:4 *One* **generation passeth away, and** *another* **generation cometh: but the earth abideth for ever.**

The Earth actually belongs to man. We want to escape earth because of sin and wickedness, but God created the earth for man.

Psalms 115:16 The heaven, *even* **the heavens,** *are* **the LORD'S: but the earth hath he given to the children of men.**

Psalms 8:6 Thou madest him to have dominion over the works of thy hands; thou hast put all *things* **under his feet:**

God desires to reveal His purposes and plans to those who have been weaned from the breast of the institutionalized church and have grown teeth to chew on meat. There must be a complete shifting in this hour to embrace God's new order. We must have new bottles in order to drink from the new wine of the Holy Spirit. We have learned from the scripture that you cannot put new wine in old wine skins: the old bottles will burst.

Luke 5:37 And no man putteth new wine into old bottles; else the new wine will burst the bottles, and be spilled, and the bottles shall perish.

The Holy Spirit orchestrates times and seasons for the Church to experience a unity with God. The worst place to be is where God used to be. This is what happened to the scribes and Pharisees; they refused to shift with the time. They were still holding on to Old Testament wineskins of Judaism. When Jesus came on the scene to establish a new move, just as it was then, so it is today, it is hard to shift when you are not ready to change. One thing that is hard to understand is All believers are ministers. Ministry is not for a selected few. Another truth that is difficult to comprehend is all can prophesy, regardless of whom you are male or female, young or old, rich or poor, all can operate in a prophetic realm. The 16th Century emphasized the priesthood of all believers. The Azusa revival in the 20th century emphasized the Holy Spirit baptism and speaking in tongues for all believers. The work of the clergy is not just for a selected few. All believers can cast out devils, heal the sick, and do the work that Jesus did on the earth.

John 14:12 Verily, verily, I say unto you, He that believeth on me, the works that I do shall he do also; and greater *works* than these shall he do; because I go unto my Father.

This is the hour of the Apostolic prophetical anointing. This does not mean that because you operate in a particular function that you are called to that particular office; however, it simply means that there is a need for the Apostolic prophetical anointing to be released in a place or a person where God is expanding His dominion. The Apostolic prophetical word releases a creative fresh word that prepares a people for new wine skins. Old wineskins are rigid and inflexible resistant to change.

The Kingdom of God brings about radical and progressive transitions in which revelation knowledge unfolds. Revelation is a knowledge that has always been but not seen before; it is a sudden burst of insight. Revelation is based on timing. I believe that revelation produces promotion as Joseph received revelation concerning Pharaoh's dream

Genesis 41:16 And Joseph answered Pharaoh, saying, *It is* not in me: God shall give Pharaoh an answer of peace.

Genesis 41:37-43 ³⁷And the thing was good in the eyes of Pharaoh, and in the eyes of all his servants. ³⁸And Pharaoh said unto his servants, Can we find *such a one* as this *is*, a man in whom the Spirit of God *is*? ³⁹And Pharaoh said

unto Joseph, Forasmuch as God hath showed thee all this, *there is* none so discreet and wise as thou *art*: ⁴⁰Thou shalt be over my house, and according unto thy word shall all my people be ruled: only in the throne will I be greater than thou. ⁴¹And Pharaoh said unto Joseph, See, I have set thee over all the land of Egypt. ⁴²And Pharaoh took off his ring from his hand, and put it upon Joseph's hand, and arrayed him in vestures of fine linen, and put a gold chain about his neck; ⁴³And he made him to ride in the second chariot which he had; and they cried before him, Bow the knee: and he made him *ruler* over all the land of Egypt.

Revelation is an answer of peace, known to God, and shown unto man particularly in a critical time. Revelation is an opportunity to share in God's wisdom, knowledge, and understanding. This revelation exalts The Kingdom of God. Problems, crises, times of pain, etc are all Karros times for God to reveal Himself. The Kingdom of God does not come with observation; it comes in demonstration. When Joseph revealed Pharaoh's dream, this was a demonstration. The church today must experience a transformation where people don't see us as insignificant "little people" religious but irrelevant to the economic recession, we are being empowered to be little gods in the earth. Until we understand, believe and act like little gods, we will only preach and teach mere words. The Cosmos needs a demonstration of the reality of the Kingdom of God. There is power and authority available to the servants of the Kingdom of God who have as Abraham separated themselves from their fathers house, (organized religion) and have left religious tradition (Kindred) and by faith they are obeying God in pursuit of the Kingdom of God. As God established covenant with Abraham so God will establish a covenant with those who are willing to transition.

Genesis 12:1-2 ¹Now the LORD had said unto Abram, Get thee out of thy country, and from thy kindred, and from thy father's house, unto a land that I will show thee: ²And I will make of thee a great nation, and I will

bless thee, and make thy name great; and thou shalt be a blessing:

Another passage of scripture that reveals the transition is found in

Romans 9:25-29 ²⁵**As he saith also in Osee, I will call them my people, which were not my people; and her beloved, which was not beloved.** ²⁶**And it shall come to pass,** *that* **in the place where it was said unto them, Ye** *are* **not my people; there shall they be called the children of the living God.** ²⁷**Esaias also crieth concerning Israel, Though the number of the children of Israel be as the sand of the sea, a remnant shall be saved:** ²⁸**For he will finish the work, and cut** *it* **short in righteousness: because a short work will the Lord make upon the earth.** ²⁹**And as Esaias said before, Except the Lord of Sabaoth had left us a seed, we had been as Sodom, and been made like unto Gomorrha. (Osee=Hosea)**

Chapter Twenty

KINGDOM BENEFITS

The Kingdom of God transcends the results of the fall of Adam and Eve. It transcends the flesh and empowers who we really are: little gods. We have received the incorruptible seed of Jesus Christ, just as Mary received Jesus Christ in her womb, we have received the same seed, which will grow in us and manifest Christ as He grows in us.

Matthew 13:31-32 ^{31}Another parable put he forth unto them, saying, The kingdom of heaven is like to a grain of mustard seed, which a man took, and sowed in his field: ^{32}Which indeed is the least of all seeds: but when it is grown, it is the greatest among herbs, and becometh a tree, so that the birds of the air come and lodge in the branches thereof.

In the past, we have placed emphasis upon prayer, faith, love, holiness, charismatic, Pentecostal, etc. We have accepted these as the end within themselves, these are simply seeds and the emphasis should not be on the seeds but on the harvest. As we allow the seed to grow in us, the results will be the fruit of the spirit, which we see in **Galatians 5:22-23.** We will begin to move like the King. The results will be so transforming until men and women will see Christ in us the hope of glory.

Galatians 4:19 My little children, of whom I travail in birth again until Christ be formed in you,

When Christ is formed in us, the Kingdom of God is revealed transcending the physical life of the flesh. The bible said the last enemy to be defeated is death. Just as Jesus conquered death by resurrection power, that power progressively grows in us: the corporate body. There is a necessity to comprehend the resurrection power of the corporate body.

Ephesians 4:11-13 [11]And he gave some, apostles; and some, prophets; and some, evangelists; and some, pastors and teachers; [12]For the perfecting of the saints, for the work of the ministry, for the edifying of the body of Christ: [13]Till we all come in the unity of the faith, and of the knowledge of the Son of God, unto a perfect man, unto the measure of the stature of the fulness of Christ:

The unity of the faith can only take place when Apostles and Prophets transcend institutionalized religion. They provide Revelation knowledge and fresh insight to love and embrace what we once failed to appreciate because of denominational walls. We learn to see Christ in every denomination. We breakthrough what used to divide us. It is amazing! We should never worship a memorial; it represents a movement leading us to a place in Christ. We have allowed this immaturity to become another barrier. The Kingdom of God transcends all of our methods and traditions. It transcends anything that separates us. The Kingdom must transcend everything we can embrace either the Kingdom transcends it or it is not God's Kingdom. Citizens of the Kingdom of God must learn our God surpasses everything and anything we label. The unity of the faith brings a progressive move of healing and health to the body; suddenly the incurable becomes curable and the impossible becomes possible.

Chapter Twenty-One

THE APOSTOLIC/
THE KINGDOM OF GOD

The Kingdom of God and the Apostolic Church are connected. When we talk about the Apostolic church, we need to understand that the Apostolic church is the Ecclesia, the called out ones from the world. This church is designed by God to be the vehicle of the Kingdom of God: a resource. The Apostolic church is separated not only from the world but also from the world in the church. The Apostolic church separates herself from cold, dead, religiosity realizing that old wine skins will never be a container for the new wine. The Apostolic church always patterns herself as the Kingdom of God. The Apostolic church of today looks at the Antioch church of yesterday in the book of Acts as a role model for today. The Apostolic church must never become the prima donna of Christianity and by so doing, steal the glory of the Kingdom of God which often happens when the church reaches mega status or television puts its spotlight on our leaders. It is at this point that many churches become untouchable and bathe themselves in pride. They become unaccountable to anyone. The Apostolic church does not measure its growth by size but by quality of the Spirit. Had Jesus based His ministry by today's standards of size, the Son of God's ministry would have certainly been classified a failure! The Apostolic church wears no title, no labels, accepts no walls, has no racial distinctions, is without male or female gender, and it is without bias of economic standards. It lives by faith and pursues the Kingdom of God with a passion. This church is the universal church that Jesus Christ will accept as His bride. Many churches are not willing to pay the price and therefore they become as the rich young ruler.

Luke 18:18-24 **[18]And a certain ruler asked him, saying, Good Master, what shall I do to inherit eternal life? [19]And Jesus said unto him, Why callest thou me good? none *is* good, save one, *that is*, God. [20]Thou knowest the commandments, Do not commit adultery, Do not kill, Do not steal, Do not bear false witness, Honour thy father and thy mother. [21]And he said, All these have I kept from my youth up. [22]Now when Jesus heard these things, he said unto him, Yet lackest thou one thing: sell all that thou hast, and distribute unto the poor, and thou shalt have treasure in heaven: and come, follow me. [23]And when he heard this, he was very sorrowful: for he was very rich. [24]And when Jesus saw that he was very sorrowful, he said, How hardly shall they that have riches enter into the kingdom of God!**

Many churches are lacking something. The major problem is they are not ready to change. The church that the Holy Spirit is now selecting as the Bride of Christ must repent (CHANGE). Many churches have reached such a successful status according to the world standards. They are the untouchables. They build their own kingdoms and therefore compete with God. They refuse new wineskins. This church will never be glorified in this hour. God is calling a people out of a people for His glory. The Apostolic church has a very important task. It must emulate the Kingdom of God. People should be able to see a miniature replica of the Kingdom of God in all that we do. This church will never accept mediocrity. This church believes excellence is the only acceptable worship and praise that we do in our daily lives not just on Sundays but all that we do should reveal worship and praise to the King of Glory. Excellence is the highest standard of quality that should be offered to a king.

Therefore, the Apostolic church always maintains a quality control that takes precedence in everything we do. Nothing is done out of tradition but must be done based upon the Will of God. Much is practiced in our churches out of repetition without careful concern (**Is this the will of God for this church at this time?**) How often do we clone particularly if we believe another church is successful? We must be sensitive to the fact that our Father has a distinct purpose, will, and design for each individual church. In addition, each one of us must recognize that the call of God is to be fulfilled according to the vision, which God has chosen for His church. What works in one place might be a disaster in another place. Just as one person's prescription may heal one but kill the next one. Each church should be autonomous and allow the Holy Spirit to orchestrate the Will of God for that local church. Just as each one of us is an individual, so the church must be individually governed and sustained by the Will of God. We are unique, gifted, favored and anointed by the Holy Spirit. I have found it is more prevalent many times for churches to mimic one another. But this is dangerous because we missed our calling. Apostles are more concerned about hearing from God more than anything else. Hearing takes more precedence that even praying. Faith does not come by praying, it comes by hearing-

Romans 10:17 So then faith *cometh* by hearing, and hearing by the word of God.

To hear from God is crucial to everyone.

THE APOSTLE

Leaders should know the distinct difference between the Apostle, the Bishop and the pastor. These are not just offices but positions that the Holy Spirit uses to empower or to shepherd. These offices or positions should be considered as foundation gifts for the body of Christ. These five offices are necessary for the maturity, the training, and equipping of the saints to do the work of ministry so as they are built up in the Word of God. They will become the Word of God made flesh: The Rhema. In the past, many people felt this was blasphemy but when we comprehend the purpose of the Holy Spirit, we understand the five-fold ministry is to equip, build up and empower us to manifest Christ in the earth. There are many theologians that teach that the office of Apostle and Prophet are irrelevant today; however, I believe the apostle and prophet are foundation ministries which Jesus Christ Himself is the chief cornerstone. There is no place in scripture where these two offices would no longer be needed. There are many who fail to note that these offices are critical to fulfilling the prayer of Jesus: Thy Kingdom come on earth as it is in heaven. The church is only the vehicle of the Kingdom of God. It is a resource of the Kingdom of God. The Apostle and the prophet are anointed and appointed to steer the church to the Kingdom of God. When we refer to the church, I am not talking about a building but a people who the Holy Spirit has called out of the world to fulfill a Kingdom of God purpose. **St. Luke 11:2. 1 Timothy 3:1 This *is* a true saying, If a man desire the office of a bishop, he desireth a good work.** Notice the emphasis "If a man desire, he desires a good work". Twice the two words are mentioned repetitiously, therefore we can readily see this office is different from **Ephesians 4:11, "And he gave some, apostles; and some, prophets; and some, evangelists; and some, pastors and teachers."** These offices are given by the Holy Spirit. The office of the bishop has been misunderstood and many times this office has been given the same operation as the apostle, which is completely different when we search the scriptures. One thing is perfectly clear; the Bishop can desire his position while the Apostles' office is a chosen office by the Holy Spirit. In **Colossians 1:1**, Paul mentions he was an Apostle by the Will of God and his spiritual son Timothy confirms this. Now read **I Timothy 1:1, "Paul, an apostle of Jesus Christ by the commandment of God our Saviour, and Lord Jesus Christ, which is our hope."** In **Titus 1:1**, Paul states his apostleship of Jesus Christ is according to the faith of God's elect. In **Ephesians 1:1**, Paul states his apostolic calling was by the Will of God. In **I Peter 1**, Peter states his apostolic calling was of Jesus Christ.

The office of the Apostle is throughout the New Testament, while the office of the bishop is mentioned six times in the New

Testament; the apostle, apostleship and apostles are mentioned over 85 times. While the bishop's office is certainly an office to be honored and respected; however, it should be understood that it is an office. However, the scripture states in **1 Timothy 3:2-7 ²A bishop then must be blameless, the husband of one wife, vigilant, sober, of good behaviour, given to hospitality, apt to teach; ³Not given to wine, no striker, not greedy of filthy lucre; but patient, not a brawler, not covetous; ⁴One that ruleth well his own house, having his children in subjection with all gravity; ⁵(For if a man know not how to rule his own house, how shall he take care of the church of God?) ⁶Not a novice, lest being lifted up with pride he fall into the condemnation of the devil. ⁷Moreover he must have a good report of them which are without; lest he fall into reproach and the snare of the devil.** Today however many believe the office of the bishop should be genderless while the apostle is historically genderless. Junia was a female apostle in history. **Romans 16:7**.

Galatians 3:28, 29, "²⁸There is neither Jew nor Greek, there is neither bond nor free, there is neither male nor female: for ye are all one in Christ Jesus. ²⁹And if ye be Christ's, then are ye Abraham's seed, and heirs according to the promise."

The office of Bishop should be regarded as an overseer, one who sets things in order. This position in **Philippians 1:1**, places the Bishops and deacons together. Also in **I Timothy 3:7-8**, the criteria and qualifications place the bishop and deacons together in qualifications. This however does not mean the Bishop and Deacon are to work together in uniformity but in unity of purpose for the well-being of the Church. This office differs from the Apostle as the bishop operates in oversight of ministries. This office however is not a Kingdom of God position to manifest Christ's power and authority in the earth. As we shall see also that the Apostolic anointing extends beyond the Spiritual sphere while Bishops operate in a spiritual environment only. The office of bishop is often a religious position while the apostle is anointed to establish a relationship with Christ's purpose and Will. The Will of

God is to make the kingdoms of the earth His dominion. Therefore, Apostles are often entrepreneurs as well as Spiritual Fathers. Bishops do not venture beyond the spiritual ministries most of the time.

Apostles ordain elders. This was an apostolic charge. **Titus 1:5**	
Apostles reform and bring change.	Bishops often do not initiate change.
Apostles teach, preach, set and clarify doctrine.	Bishops often fulfill this mandate.
Apostles release revelation concerning the plans and purposes of God-Apostles easily flow in the prophetical, dreams visions and revelation knowledge.	Bishops seldom flow in this area.
Apostles raise up and establish teams. Apostles and prophets utilize teams.	Where Bishops do not.
Apostles oversee churches.	Bishops are very active in oversight-This is their element. Apostles do it but operate this function differently by the Kingdom principals.
Apostles confirm and strengthen local churches. Apostles do this by the Holy Spirit operations and Kingdom of God principles.	Bishops are often leaders of tradition. The Apostolic anointing being released upon a congregation can release a paradigm shift.
Apostles bring judgment and correction.	Bishops were not referenced with the Holy Spirit. Read **Acts 5:1-12** to see what the Apostle Peter said to Ananias and his wife Sapphira.

Apostles defend the faith. This is clearly seen in the Acts of the Apostles not the acts of the bishops.	
Apostles gather. This is also evident in **Acts 4:6**	
Apostles establish. **Acts 16:5**	
Apostles lay foundation. **Eph. 2:20**	
Apostles root out, tear down, throw down, destroy, build and plant. Jesus did this when he walked the earth and so can we. The apostolic symbol is the sword.	
Apostles water. **I. Cor. 3:6**	
Apostles release and activate. Apostles bless the poor. **Acts 6:1-3** This was where the office of deacons took place-the plight of the poor empowered apostolic wisdom.	Bishops often are charitable.
Apostles help to empower and mature the saints. The Book of **Acts 10:28.** Maturity is when you can accept every man regardless of race or color, rich or poor, Jew or Gentile, bond or free, male or female. True equality is a sign of maturity.	

Apostles assist in the full release of the Holy Spirit. The Apostle Peter in **Acts 11:15** stated, **"And as I began to speak the Holy Ghost fell on them as on us at the beginning."**	
Apostles maintain order. **Acts 4:13, "Now when they saw the boldness of Peter and John** (Apostles) **and perceived they were unlearned and ignorant men, they marveled; and they took knowledge of them, that they had been with Jesus."**	
Apostles impart. Impartation is clearly seen in **Acts 3:6**. The lame man is healed by Peter and John.	
Apostles bring strategies to the church. The entire book of acts is a book of Apostolic strategies.	
Apostles operate in signs, wonders and miracles. **Acts 5:12**	
Apostles flow in the supernatural as a natural element.	Bishops are many times limited in operating in the supernatural.
Apostles can remit sins. This is a promise Jesus stated in **St. John 20:22,23**, when he had said this he breathed on them and said to them, Receive ye the Holy Ghost Whosoever sins you remit, they are remitted unto them; whosoever sins you retain, they are retained.	
Apostles can be versatile. The versatility is the work of the Holy Ghost to reach the total man- Spirit, Soul and Body.	

The Apostolic anointing can operate politically as it did for Joseph in Egypt. I believe this office can bring favor and abundance to nations. This anointing can be released upon entrepreneurial-minded people, with a market place empowerment anointing. This empowerment anointing can expand the Kingdom of God into education, health, business, politics, science, sports, fashions and entertainment. Apostolic favor can bring salvation to many people who find that they can pursue a career in another field beside religion and they can still be in the Will of God. They can still be in ministry for the King of Glory. I believe God wants to expand upon this empowerment TRUTH TODAY.

Psalms 112:1-6 **¹ Praise ye the LORD. Blessed** *is* **the man** *that* **feareth the LORD,** *that* **delighteth greatly in his commandments.**
² His seed shall be mighty upon earth: the generation of the upright shall be blessed.
³ Wealth and riches shall be in his house: and his righteousness endureth for ever.
⁴ Unto the upright there ariseth light in the darkness: he is gracious, and full of compassion, and righteous.
⁵ A good man showeth favour, and lendeth: he will guide his affairs with discretion.
⁶ Surely he shall not be moved for ever: the righteous shall be in everlasting remembrance.

Proverbs 13:22 A good man leaveth an inheritance to his children's children: and the wealth of the sinner is laid up for the just.

The Kingdom of God has never experienced layoffs, recession, foreclosures and bankruptcy. I believe the marketplace apostolic anointing is an answer to bring significant change to a dismal future with the economy for the apostolic church. When Israel left Egypt the bible states, they left with 400 years of back wages. They spoiled Egypt. I believe this is transfer time of wealth to the righteous, which are willing to walk in apostolic wisdom. The apostolic anointing is multifaceted, which causes them to be able to move into many areas, to expand the

Kingdom of God. This anointing is very influential and represents a wide range of wisdom and authority. Where the apostle walks, the grace of God is manifested. All gifts operate by faith. However, when the apostle walks in the fullness of their calling there is a greater dimension of released faith than seen in other grace gifts. The apostolic anointing still encounters obstacles and setbacks, but memory and maturity won't let them settle for less. They are submitted to the King of Glory; this qualifies them to resist the devil and watch him take off.

James 4:7 Submit yourselves therefore to God. Resist the devil, and he will flee from you.

Joshua 11:1-8 **¹And it came to pass, when Jabin king of Hazor had heard those things, that he sent to Jobab king of Madon, and to the king of Shimron, and to the king of Achshaph, ²And to the kings that were on the north of the mountains, and of the plains south of Chinneroth, and in the valley, and in the borders of Dor on the west, ³And to the Canaanite on the east and on the west, and to the Amorite, and the Hittite, and the Perizzite, and the Jebusite in the mountains, and to the Hivite under Hermon in the land of Mizpeh. ⁴And they went out, they and all their hosts with them, much people, even as the sand that is upon the sea shore in multitude, with horses and chariots very many. ⁵And when all these kings were met together, they came and pitched together at the waters of Merom, to fight against Israel. ⁶And the LORD said unto Joshua, Be not afraid because of them: for tomorrow about this time will I deliver them up all slain before Israel: thou shalt hough their horses, and burn their chariots with fire. ⁷So Joshua came, and all the people of war with him, against them by the waters of Merom suddenly; and they fell upon them. ⁸And the LORD delivered them into the hand of Israel, who smote them, and chased them unto great Zidon, and unto Misrephothmaim, and unto the valley of Mizpeh eastward; and they smote them, until they left them none remaining.**

Chapter Twenty-Two

THE PROPHET IN THE HOUSE

2 Kings 3:11 But Jehoshaphat said, Is there not here a prophet of the LORD, that we may enquire of the LORD by him? And one of the king of Israel's servants answered and said, Here is Elisha the son of Shaphat, which poured water on the hands of Elijah.

Next to the Apostolic anointing is the prophetical anointing. As we spoke earlier everybody in the house can prophecy.

1 Corinthians 14:5 I would that ye all spake with tongues, but rather that ye prophesied: for greater is he that prophesieth than he that speaketh with tongues, except he interpret, that the church may receive edifying.

There are many that interpret prophecy in

1 Corinthians 14:1 Follow after charity, and desire spiritual gifts, but rather that ye may prophesy.

They substitute prophecy to preaching. Although to preach is a form of prophesying but to prophesy transcends preaching; it is revelation knowledge demonstrated.

1 Corinthians 14:24-26 **²⁴But if all prophesy, and there come in one that believeth not, or one unlearned, he is convinced of all, he is judged of all: ²⁵And thus are the secrets of his heart made manifest; and so falling down on his face he will worship God, and report that God is in you of a truth.
²⁶How is it then, brethren? when ye come together, every one of you hath a psalm, hath a doctrine, hath a tongue, hath a revelation, hath an interpretation. Let all things be done unto edifying.**

Prophecy flows into the deeper life of the spirit, the wisdom, knowledge, and understanding of the Lord of Host. One of the attributes of God is He is omniscient, which means He is unlimited in knowledge. God is absolute in His intelligence. He knows everything there is to know. He is infinite; man is finite, which means man is limited in wisdom, and knowledge. He is always limited. Man can only handle a fragmented amount of God's infinite intelligence. The creator's wisdom is beyond comprehension but God being willing to manifest His love and grace allows man to demonstrate in an abbreviated version, the supernatural intelligence of God.

After the fall, mankind needed priests, prophets and kings. Previously, these offices were the only ones that were anointed. The priest offered man's sacrifice for sin. The high priest went into the Holy of Holies once per year. The priest represented man to God; the prophet represented God to men. The prophet spoke through men's lips, revealing God's Will and wisdom to His people. In Old Testament days, the prophet was a mandate for the children of Israel, Eli the priest, refused to correct his children. God raised up a prophet called Samuel who was a type of the presence of God. The office was so vital until The Prophets built a school of the prophets. This was done that Israel would always have a succession of prophets throughout generations. Israel recognized the necessity of prophets yesterday. The church should learn from Israel the importance of prophecy. In Old Testament days, the prophet saw God to empower them to perform miracles, signs and wonders. The prophet represented God's intelligence and God's ability. Today God still desires to speak to His church corporately and locally. The church, being the vehicle of the Kingdom of God, must always have clear directions. The prophet represents a spiritual compass or navigation system. They are God's spokesperson, bringing perfection, empowerment, and wisdom. This office works with the apostolic anointing to bring transition to the body of Christ. Apostles and prophets are sensitive to recognize the need for consistent changes the body must make.

1 Corinthians 14:3 But he that prophesieth speaketh unto men *to* edification, and exhortation, and comfort.

The church always needs edification, exhortation, and comfort. The prophet is a type of the cloud by day and the pillar of fire by night to signal transition time. Some prophets see visions and hear the voice of the Lord, while others only hear. Prophecy can be birthed through dreams, visions, and revelation. Inspiration can result from prophetical anointings. Everybody can prophesy in the entire church and not be called to the office of prophet. Many times God desires to declare a Rhema Word in the midst of a local church service, but because of lack of confidence in ourselves or fear, we neglect to release a Word from God that could strengthen an individual, or the corporate group of believers. The more a person is allowed to exercise this gift, the more comfortable they will become in using it. This gift should always have a seasoned prophet in the midst to judge not condemn, which could crush the individual and quench the Spirit of the student.

1 Corinthians 14:29-33 [29]Let the prophets speak two or three, and let the other judge. [30]If *any thing* be revealed to another that sitteth by, let the first hold his peace. [31]For ye may all prophesy one by one, that all may learn, and all may be comforted. [32]And the spirits of the prophets are subject to the prophets. [33]For God is not *the author* of confusion, but of peace, as in all churches of the saints.

Prophecy can be spoken or sung. If the person is gifted to sing, this can be inspirational. If you are not gifted or talented to sing,

The Kingdom Shift

you would hinder and limit the message being conveyed. You could embarrass yourself and block the flow of the Spirit. Prophetical training can birth prophetical teams, which can move the church to another level in Spiritual intelligence. This empowerment team can lift loads off apostles, pastors and church leaders. This team can be productive in intercessory prayer group empowerment. Praying and not hearing is like a one-way conversation. God desires to speak to His people to build faith, to confirm, to bring correction, and to build up. Student prophets should never attempt to bring Judgment, to root out, to tear down, even to plant. Every person should learn to abide in their calling. It is like driving: stay in your lane for safety. An experienced prophet can work as a team with the apostle to bring correction, discipline, to destroy and build. Student prophets can learn journaling, dream study, how to know the voice of the Lord, how to meditate in the Word of God and learning the times and seasons of the flowing of the Spirit. Another important lesson is mentoring which was the empowerment of Elisha. The Elijah to Elisha impartation can be life changing. It changed Elisha's life: he received a double portion of one of Israel's most influential prophets. Fathering and mentoring I have found is worth more than years of seminary training. I have chosen to eliminate discussing the pastor, evangelist and teacher because these particular gifts receive much coverage in instructions and use. It is my prayer that this writing will empower the reader to know who they are and what they can do as they shift from "churchianity" to Kingdom truth.

ENLARGE YOUR THINKING, STRETCH YOUR IMAGINATION, SPARE NOT LENGTHEN YOUR DREAMS STRENGTHEN YOUR MIND IN THE WORD OF GOD. YOU CAN SEE A NEW FUTURE. YOU CAN BREAKTHROUGH TO NEW HORIZONS AS YOU SHALL INHABIT THE KINGDOM OF GOD. THIS IS YOUR HOUR TO TAKE THE KINGDOM SAITH THE LORD OF HOST.

Other Books by Paul A. Thomas

Potiphar's House: Process to Your Promotion

Supporting The Leaders Around You: A Manual For Local Church Leadership

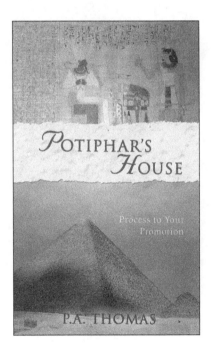

CPSIA information can be obtained
at www.ICGtesting.com
Printed in the USA
LVHW092320150120
643806LV00001B/254